MY SHOT

ALSO BY ELENA DELLE DONNE

Hoops

Elle of the Ball

Full-Court Press

Out of Bounds

ELENA DELLE DONNE

with SARAH DURAND

MY SHOT

BALANCING IT ALL AND STANDING TALL

SIMON & SCHUSTER BFYR

NEW YORK LONDON TORONTO SYDNEY NEW DELHI

SIMON & SCHUSTER BFYR

An imprint of Simon & Schuster Children's Publishing Division
1230 Avenue of the Americas, New York, New York 10020
This work is a memoir. It reflects the author's present recollections
of (her) experiences over a period of years.
SIMON & SCHUSTER BFYR is a trademark of Simon & Schuster, Inc.
For information about special discounts for bulk purchases, please contact Simon &
Schuster Special Sales at 1-866-506-1949 or business@simonandschuster.com.
The Simon & Schuster Speakers Bureau can bring authors to your live event. For more
information or to book an event, contact the Simon & Schuster Speakers Bureau at
1-866-248-3049 or visit our website at www.simonspeakers.com.
Also available in a SIMON & SCHUSTER BFYR hardcover edition
Book design by Krista Vossen
The text for this book was set in Minion Pro.
Manufactured in the United States of America
First SIMON & SCHUSTER BFYR paperback edition March 2019
2 4 6 8 10 9 7 5 3 1
The Library of Congress has cataloged the hardcover edition as follows:
Names: Donne, Elena Delle, author. | Durand, Sarah, author.
Title: My shot : balancing it all and standing tall / Elena Delle Donne,
with Sarah Durand.
Description: First Edition. | New York : Simon & Schuster Books for Young Readers,
[2018] | Audience: Ages: 12 up. | Audience: Grades: 7 to 8.
Identifiers: LCCN 2017027207|
ISBN 9781534412286 (Hardcover) | ISBN 9781534412293 (pbk) |
ISBN 9781534412309 (eBook)
Subjects: LCSH: Delle Donne, Elena,—Juvenile literature. | Women basketball
  players—United States—Biography—Juvenile literature. | Women's National
  Basketball Association—History—Juvenile literature.
Classification: LCC GV884.D65 D66 2018 | DDC 796.323092 [B]—dc23
LC record available at https://lccn.loc.gov/2017027207

To my wife, Amanda,
for giving me the courage to unapologetically be me.
The fog on the journey lifted the day our paths met.
—E. D. D.

CONTENTS

Introduction

Part One // Foul Trouble

Part Two // Rebound

Part Four // Slam Dunk

Introduction

I hate basketball.

Those three words were the last thing anyone ever expected me to say to myself. After all, I'd decided when I was six that I wanted to be the best player in the country, and I'd worked toward that goal each day since. In middle school I'd forced myself out of bed at six a.m. to run—rain or shine, every single day—shot free throws after practice till the sun went down, and then lifted weights at home on weekends. I'd been named the nation's top female high school recruit during my senior year, and when the media had called me a female LeBron James, I'd been honored. Then the University of Connecticut—considered by many to be the best women's basketball program in the world—had offered me a full ride, and I'd given them an enthusiastic yes. I knew I was one of the best young basketball players in the country, so why was I ready to walk away from all of it? Especially when I'd barely given college sports a chance?

Because I hate basketball. And I never want to play again.

It was June 2008, and I was just about to start classes at UConn. Because the women's basketball team trained during the summer, a few days earlier I'd driven with my family from Wilmington, Delaware, to Storrs, Connecticut, moved into a dorm, and enrolled in classes for the summer term. That night I was going to meet my teammates on the UConn women's basketball team for the first time. *This is what I've been working for since I could hold a basketball,* I told myself. *And you can't get any better than UConn.*

From the second I kissed my family good-bye, though, I was more miserable than I'd ever been in my life. And when I pulled on a T-shirt and a pair of baggy shorts, laced up my shoes, and headed toward a pickup game the seniors had pulled together to welcome all of us, I felt even worse.

"Hi, Elena," said one of the captains when I walked up to her and a group of my teammates. "It's so good to see you. Welcome. Geno asked me to tell you personally that he hopes you're ready for a great season."

I smiled. "I am. Thank you."

Geno Auriemma was the UConn head coach, and he was a basketball legend. Before he'd gotten to UConn in 1985, the women's team had had only one winning season. Within two years he'd turned the program around, and by 1995, UConn went undefeated and won the National Collegiate Athletic Association (NCAA) women's title. He'd led the Huskies to five national championship wins since then and had become one of the most famous coaches in Division I NCAA basketball history—for women *and* men's teams. Playing under him wasn't just a privilege; it was an honor. So why did the thought of it make me feel sick?

Because I can't face up to the fact that I can't stand basketball anymore.

Still, I promised myself I'd work hard during that first game. My teammates deserved that. They consisted of girls I'd met at tournaments around the country, women I'd played with at invitationals, and names I'd only heard whispered in hushed tones in the locker room. I'm 6'5", and I was taller than almost all of them, but there were plenty of six footers on the Husky squad. Off the basketball court, I knew they'd felt different and out of place all their lives, just like me. I knew they'd been stared at. When I was three, someone stopped my mom in the grocery store and said, "An eight-year-old shouldn't be using a pacifier!" These girls could relate to situations like that. Probably all of them had turned to basketball because it was a safe haven. The court was a place where tall girls weren't just normal; we were the *stars*, and our parents, teachers, and coaches had all lovingly pushed us down a path where we could shine. Basketball was written in our DNA, and we excelled at it. That was why we'd made it our life mission. Sure, it was what we told ourselves we were expected to do, but it didn't matter, because we did it so well. We were *the best*. What could possibly be wrong with that?

What's wrong is that I'm exhausted. Practicing so hard for so long has taken everything out of me.

Plus, I missed my family—terribly. My sister, Lizzie, is six years older than I am. She was born blind and deaf and was diagnosed with cerebral palsy not long after she went home from the hospital. When she was a toddler, doctors discovered she also had autism. Lizzie could understand the outside world only through her senses of touch and smell. A hot, stinky gym and hard bleacher seats make her uncomfortable, so she'd been to only a handful of my basketball games. She hadn't seen me make my eightieth consecutive successful free throw—a record that still stands today—nor had she heard the screams of the crowd at any of my All-State games. If I did well on the Huskies, she'd never know me as one of the best basketball players in college hoops. But that didn't matter. She thought of me as part of *her* team—and that had nothing to do with basketball.

I miss Lizzie, I thought. *If I'm here, I can't hold her hands. She can't smell the sweat on me after practice. She can't feel the wind through her hair as we walk around my parents' yard. When I'm with her, she doesn't expect me to make a perfect shot or a perfect defensive play. Lizzie just wants to love me and spend time with me, and that can't happen if I'm at UConn.*

I heard a whistle blow, and I grabbed a basketball from the sideline bench and jogged with my brand-new teammates out onto the court. As we circled up, I looked at everyone's faces. Some girls were smiling, and some were nervously biting their lips. Some had wide-open eyes, and others were shuffling from one foot to the other. But all of us clutched our basketballs tight, waiting for someone to start talking.

One of the team captains finally broke the silence. "There are some new faces and some old familiar ones here today.

Some of you have traveled thousands of miles to get here, and others live right down the road. You all come from different places and have different kinds of families, but what ties you together is your passion for basketball. Geno and the entire coaching staff are going to demand that from you all year. More than hard work or natural talent, they want you to have *passion*."

I listened to her closely, and when she was finished speaking, I dribbled the ball, made a few baskets, and threw myself into the toughest pickup game of my life. When it was over, my muscles were screaming, and I knew I'd been physically challenged in a way I'd never been in high school. Geno Auriemma and the UConn women's basketball team were ready to demand the mental, emotional, and physical excellence that had made them the best squad in the country, and I understood that if I wanted to give them that, I had to lead with passion.

Deep in my heart, though, I realized the sad truth. *Passion's not something I can give them*, I thought. *I'll fake it today and tomorrow, but I really, truly hate this sport. I've burned out.*

After I peeled off my sweaty clothes and stepped into a steaming hot shower, I paused for a minute and made my decision. I was going to quit basketball. Not just for the season but forever. Elena Delle Donne might have been the most sought after and celebrated women's high school basketball recruit in the country, but she was going home.

PART ONE
FOUL TROUBLE

Chapter One

Home

The thing about being different is that you don't really realize you are until someone points it out to you. My mom is 6'2" and my dad is 6'6", so I can't remember a time when they weren't ducking to get through doorways or smiling at silly, obvious comments like, "Boy, you're so tall!" They always towered above other people, but when I was little, that seemed normal because they were my family. And my family was my whole world.

I was born in late 1989 in the suburbs of Wilmington, Delaware. I was the third of three kids, below my brother, Gene, and my sister, Lizzie. Gene is three years older than me, and he's always been a goofball. Nothing was ever too serious for him to laugh at. Even when he played high school basketball at Salesianum School, an all-boys Catholic school, and people taunted him at the free throw line by saying, "Your sister's a better player than you!" Gene would just smile. Nothing rattled him. Sometimes he'd miss the shot (I actually *was* better than him!), but he didn't care. His goal in life was to make others around him happy, so he never pitied himself.

I sometimes wonder if he decided at a very young age to be optimistic and never let anything drag him down, because of Lizzie. Gene is three years younger than Lizzie, and he more than anyone else lived through her pain. Early on he didn't have a sibling to talk to when my dad was struggling to lift Lizzie from her wheelchair and help her walk across the room, or when she was being wheeled into one of the thirty surgeries she's had because of her conditions. Most of those operations were to cure her blindness—and all of them failed—but one of his first memories related to Lizzie's long, painful recovery after a spinal surgery she had when she was seven. For three years, till I came along, Gene was all alone with two parents who struggled twenty-four hours a day to give their disabled child love and top-notch medical care. I think he saw all of that and decided to turn outward rather than inward. He wanted to see Mom and Dad laugh rather than cry.

Luckily, that wasn't always so hard. Dad went to work before the sun came up and didn't get home till dinner was on the table, but he was always ready to play with us. We had a game we called "knee football," where he'd crawl around on his knees while Gene and I—both standing—tried to tackle him. He rubbed my back till I fell asleep, and then he'd stay up all night constructing the K'NEX roller coasters I hadn't been able to finish before bedtime. Mom might have spent her days taking Lizzie to doctor appointments and physical therapy while Dad worked hard helping to build his father's real estate development company, but she always woke us up with a delicious, homemade breakfast. She was first in line to pick me up at school, and on the rare few times when she was late, I always assumed something terrible had happened. She was on top of every detail in our lives and made sure to spend quality time with each of us, which must have been a real struggle given all that Lizzie was going through.

Cerebral palsy is a chronic, incurable condition. Doctors refer to it as a movement disorder, which means it affects the muscles and prevents a person's body from working the way it's supposed to. Doctors and scientists often don't know exactly what causes it, but they do understand that the problems stem from a baby's developing brain. Sometime during pregnancy, childbirth, or early childhood, a part of the brain doesn't come together the way it should, and parents might discover that their baby doesn't sit up when he or she is supposed to, has trouble making sounds, or shakes for no reason.

Doctors knew something was wrong with Lizzie right away. From the moment she came into the world, it was obvious she couldn't see, because her eyes wouldn't focus, and just a few days later, she didn't pass her hearing test. When she was a few months old, she still couldn't hold her head up, and doctors worried she never would. When she finally walked, she couldn't do it on her own, and she still needs one of us to guide her. These days she usually gets around in a wheelchair, which we have to push. She goes to a special-needs facility called the Mary Campbell Center from nine to three during the week, and after Mom picks her up and takes her home, she hangs out on her couch in our living room with her babysitter or one of us.

Cerebral palsy is pretty common—about one out of every five hundred babies is diagnosed with it—and, luckily, the treatments are good, because the medical community spends a tremendous amount of time and money researching them. Lizzie has always had a team of doctors on hand, as well as the same wonderful babysitter for more than twenty years, and our focus has always been on making her happy rather than "fixing" her. What I mean is that we've always looked forward rather than backward. Lizzie is never viewed as a problem or a lost cause—we do *everything* to make her life better. How could I ever see her as something hopeless? I'm her sister, and I love her with every bone in my body.

I often wonder if, like Gene, I became the person I am as a reaction to Lizzie. Because I've always spent so much time with her, I know she has shaped my adult decisions, but part of me thinks I was changing and responding to her the moment I came home from the hospital. Caring for her was the focus of our lives at home, so it just makes sense that I'd always be aware of her, constantly making choices based on how it would affect her and my family dynamic.

I remember sitting in a physical therapy appointment with my mom and dad when I was about five, playing with some toys that I'd picked up from the waiting room. I looked up and saw my parents stretching Lizzie's legs out on the table. Lizzie wore braces, which they'd taken off, and she was grimacing as they moved and massaged her stiff muscles.

"It's okay," my mom said as she leaned down to kiss Lizzie's face. "It's almost over."

Lizzie couldn't hear anything Mom said, of course, but I like to think she could sense the vibration of Mom's voice. I know she could feel the kiss and Mom's and Dad's soft touches, but I wonder if she could feel the air come out of Mom's lungs. Mom always spoke to her, probably thinking the same thing, but it was more than that. She refused to treat Lizzie differently from me or Gene.

Lizzie's so brave, I thought. *She's doing everything she can, living her best life, in the body she was born with. So I'm going to do the same thing too.*

As a reaction to Lizzie, I gained confidence in my body's abilities early on. When I was three, I picked up a wrench and took the training wheels off my bike. My mom and dad stood inside, watching me from a window. Later that year I saw Dad, Gene, and a few of his friends playing Wiffle Ball in our backyard, and I ran outside and begged them to let me join in. They said yes, and I grabbed the big, plastic bat. Dad tossed me a slow, underhand pitch, and I knocked it into the neighbors' yard. By the end of the day, Dad was throwing the same overhand pitches he'd lob to Gene, and I hadn't missed a single one.

When I was in third grade, our gym teacher decided to teach juggling one day. Each student took turns trying to keep three balls in the air without dropping any, and all of them struggled. Then it was my turn.

"Okay, here we go," I said as I tossed one up.

For probably two minutes I didn't drop a single ball. I took to juggling right away.

I don't mean to sound like I'm bragging. Those of you who look different—like I did, being so tall—know the shame that can come with it when people stare at you or comment on your appearance. Like I said earlier, you don't realize how different you are until someone points it out to you or it becomes clear in some other obvious way. I remember at eight years old having a classmate trace my body on butcher paper and then hang it on the wall. Most kids' papers stopped before they reached the floor. Mine hit the ground and then extended a foot out into the classroom. I was humiliated, thinking, *I might as well have two heads.*

Again, my family hadn't made me feel like I was different, but when I was faced with "normal" people or when I was talked about, I felt so odd. But, like Lizzie, I somehow knew I had to deal with it, so I subconsciously convinced myself to shrug it off and stand tall—literally. I never slouched or slumped, and I wasn't clumsy. I held my body strong because I decided my heart should be that way too. Just like Lizzie's.

I don't remember exactly why I decided that I wanted to play basketball. Mom and Dad told me that I first picked up a ball when I was four, started to dribble it, and then refused to put it away for the next week. Even though I was clearly athletic, they never pushed me into sports. Dad had played basketball in high school and golf in college, and Mom had been a high school swimmer, but just because they loved sports didn't mean their kids had to. But when I was five,

Mom and Dad enrolled me in a youth basketball league at the local YMCA, and I never looked back. I started playing every chance I got. Dad set the basket outside our house at the five-foot height, moved it up a little bit every few months, and by the time I was eight, it was at the full ten-foot mark. Throughout all those years, when Dad would practice with me, he'd urge me never to change my form just so I could make a basket. He taught me the fundamentals, then made sure I never deviated from them.

A few of my parents' friends had strong feelings about me playing in an organized league, and they didn't hold back from saying something about it. "It's a good thing you got Elena started so early," one neighbor said, "because she's already so tall." Mom brushed that off. She didn't want me to feel like I *had* to play basketball because of my height. As a tall woman herself, she was aware that this kind of attitude sent a message to girls like me. It was like the world was telling us: *What else is a girl who's taller than all the boys supposed to do? She definitely can't be a ballet dancer or a gymnast!* Mom didn't believe that. She thought I could do anything I wanted, whether it was basketball or art or something else entirely. Sports—and certainly not basketball—weren't mandated, like homework or chores. She wanted me to play basketball because I chose it, and she and Dad hoped I'd have fun doing it.

I did. In fact, I didn't just like it; I was head over heels in love with it. I was also really, really good at it. When I was in second grade and Gene was in fifth, I was on his boys team, and every single one of my teammates was at least three years older than I was.

During that year's championship game, the score was tied with only a few seconds left, and Gene stole the ball. He looked down the court and threw it to me. My right hand is my money hand, but instead of going for a right-handed layup after I caught the ball, I shot with my left hand. I didn't notice Gene, but I'm sure he wanted to kill me for not taking the sure shot.

It didn't matter. *Swoosh*. The ball went in for two points, and we won the first-place trophy.

I'd saved the game, and my life in basketball had officially taken off.

Chapter Two

Growing Up in Basketball

One of the nice things about youth sports is that you don't have to take them too seriously unless you really want to. Even young kids are under such pressure these days—being interviewed for preschool, tested all through kindergarten, and shuttled from school to music lessons, then home to do hours of homework—that I think they need a place where they can kick back and have fun.

It took me a long time to realize it, but now I believe that the basketball court can be that. I coach girls' youth clinics—called the Delle Donne Academy—during the Women's National Basketball Association (WNBA) off-season, and I frequently see kids who are exhausted because of school, tests, family obligations, and after-school activities. I watch them stand nervously in front of me, worried that I'm going to criticize them for the foul they made, or yell at them to run a little harder and push themselves more.

Instead I try to make them relax with a reality check. "We're going to work really hard here," I'll say, "and you're going to make tons of mistakes. Don't worry; that means you're challenging yourself and getting out of your comfort zone. But more important than anything else you do here, we're all going to have lots of fun."

I wish I'd realized that when I was young. Right from the very start, I was too hard on myself. When I played at the Y and we'd have midafternoon games on the weekends, my mom sometimes suggested we go to the mall or shopping beforehand.

"I can't," I'd always say. "I need to stay home and conserve my energy."

Even then I was planting the seeds of my own burnout.

Mom and Dad never put pressure on me, so the intensity in my life really started by accident. My dad hired a physical therapist named John Noonan, who was a former high school point guard, to train my brother. Gene had shown such promise as a basketball player that Dad figured having a little extra help would ease him into middle school—and then high school—sports. Sure, I was really excelling in the youth leagues, but no one thought of giving me extra coaching. After all, I was only in second grade. But when I tagged along to one of John's training sessions for Gene, my dad started to feel differently.

"John," my dad said, "would you be able to train Elena, too? People just assume she's supposed to be a center or a forward because she's so tall, but I want her to see the game from the eyes of a point guard."

"Sure," said John. "When I'm finished up with Gene, let's run her through a few drills."

I ran to the bathroom to change into the gym clothes I'd brought along, and as I got dressed, I realized I was more excited than I'd ever been in my life. *My family and my youth league coaches know how good I am. But now I have a chance to shine in front of a real, live, one-on-one trainer.*

When John motioned for me to run onto the court, I began to move the way my body told me to. *Don't charge too fast,* I told myself. Like I said, tall girls usually aren't known for their grace, but when John threw a pass behind me, I caught it with both hands, then made a reverse layup. I didn't lunge or lumber; I just connected my hands with the ball and my vision with the hoop, then shot when my heart and mind told me the time was right.

The rim didn't shake and the net didn't move as the basketball passed through. When I straightened my legs and turned toward John, his mouth was wide open.

"That was amazing," he said. "You were perfect."

The few drills he'd planned turned into a full-out training session. He had me sprint up and down the court, take forty free throws (I only missed one!), and dribble through cones he'd placed strategically from the half-court line to the paint, which is the familiar term for the rectangular box underneath the basket. He tried to throw me off by tossing me bad passes, and when I caught them perfectly—and then scored—he'd make his passes even sloppier. I'd still catch them and shoot. At one point I looked up into the stands, and I could see Gene with his head on his knees like he was about to fall asleep. But my dad was grinning from ear to ear. He was right; I was moving as fast and as nimbly as a point guard and netting the ball as perfectly as the best offensive players.

"Can we stop so I can have a drink of water?" I finally asked John.

He looked at his watch and practically jumped. "Oh no. I'm so sorry. We've been practicing nonstop for forty-five minutes! I lost track of time. Yes, go get some water!"

As I sprinted toward my water bottle, which I'd left on the sideline, I realized I wasn't even tired. Sure, I was thirsty and sweating, but I felt like I was doing what I was meant to do, and doing it so well. Still, there was a little voice in my head nudging me. It was saying, *If you work a little harder, maybe you'll be perfect. Just push yourself to the limit, and you'll be the best basketball player in the world someday.*

When I was in second grade, John Noonan became my basketball trainer, and he stayed with me all throughout high school and college. Like I said before, he had been a point guard in high school, and sometimes I wonder if he knew what to do with a player like me at first. Here I was, so tall that it was clear I was going to tower over almost everyone before I even got to middle school, yet he never forced me into a particular position on the court. He never said, "You're big, so you need to block like a center does. Don't try to be too offensive or take all the shots like a guard does." He saw me as someone like Larry Bird—a tall player who was all hustle. To John, I was both an offensive and defensive player who could do anything for my team, anytime during the game.

He never pushed me too hard, though. Sure, our workouts were challenging, and he never let me quit, but he didn't put extra, needless pressure on me. He never made me feel like I wasn't good enough. Neither did my parents. Sometimes I think they just wanted me to feel normal because they already had one child who was *so* different.

But the truth was I *was* different. There was no getting around it. I was taller than every other person in my class.

"Your height is a good thing," Mom would say when I complained about it. "It's special. *You're* special."

But instead of stopping to take pride in my accomplishments, I decided to push myself harder. When I was ten, my league team went to the national championships, and even though we placed third, I scored more points than anyone on either team, and I vowed we'd win the championship soon. Two years later we did. By the time I was in eighth grade, I was playing varsity for Ursuline Academy, and I was named to the All-State team. I spent every single weekend practicing, working out, training with John, crawling out of bed to run, or traveling to tournaments, and I was doing it because I was convinced that if I didn't extend myself just a little further, someone would do better than me.

The only time I wasn't running from one place to the next was when I was with Lizzie.

Because Lizzie can't get around by herself, she has always spent a lot of time on her favorite couch. I imagine it's scary not being able to communicate or sense what's around you, so my parents, Gene, and I have always made an effort to let

Lizzie know we're close by. Since Lizzie was an infant, Mom has worn the same kind of Chanel perfume so that Lizzie can smell her when Mom walks into a room. When I was just a baby, I learned to use a type of sign language called hand-over-hand, which involves me placing my hands against Lizzie's so that I can draw out simple words and phrases that are important to her, like "sleep," "swim," or—don't laugh—"cheese." (Lizzie really loves cheese!) When all you can focus on is the touch of someone's hands or the silence of a quiet room while sitting side by side with the person you love more than anyone else, it's easy to feel at peace. Time with Lizzie was more important than being anywhere else in the world, and I loved it.

By the time I was thirteen, I wished that I loved basketball half as much. But I just didn't.

The summer after seventh grade, my team attended a weeklong camp in Chapel Hill, North Carolina, home of the University of North Carolina Tar Heels. Most people know UNC for their amazing men's basketball team, but the fact is that their women's team is equally impressive. Their head coach, Sylvia Hatchell, is the third winningest coach in the NCAA women's division—ahead of even Geno Auriemma—and she has led her team to twenty-two NCAA tournament berths out of thirty-one seasons with UNC. My team was going to scrimmage for a week with other high school squads while she and her assistant coaches observed us, and to say I was nervous was an understatement. I *had* to be the best there, so I stayed up late every night practicing.

I gave our first few games everything I had. I used the skills John had taught me and combined them with the physical strength I'd spent hours honing. That's one of the things about being good at sports; you can be strong, but you also have to be smart. John had helped me with my technical skills, and I'd practiced them again and again until they felt effortless.

At the end of one practice, Sylvia approached me.

"You're Elena, right?"

"I am," I said, blushing. "It's so good to meet you." I extended my hand to shake hers.

"I want to see you in my office."

All I could think was that I'd done something terribly wrong. I was convinced I was in deep trouble.

Instead, when I got to her office, she lavished praise on me. "I'm so impressed with you," she said. "Your skill level is way ahead of most people your age. You seem incredibly intelligent out there, and it's clear you're going to be a star."

I barely managed to get my words out. "Um, thank you. Thank you so much, Coach Hatchell."

"That's why I want to offer you a full scholarship to attend UNC and play basketball here. I know you have the rest of middle school and high school ahead of you, but after you graduate, I hope you'll come here."

At the age of thirteen, when I hadn't even grown to my full 6'5" frame, I received my first college scholarship offer. When most girls were begging their moms to go to the mall on Friday night, or dreaming of getting their learner's permits,

I was already being asked to consider where I'd go to college. Talk about pressure.

"Th-thank you," I stammered. "I'm so honored. But I need to think about this and talk to my parents. I'll let you know as soon as I can."

Coach Hatchell assured me there was no rush, and I took the rest of camp to let her offer sink in. When I went home and talked it over with my mom and dad, we decided I should tell her that I'd sit on the offer till high school. I'd say it was because settling on a college in seventh grade was just too early. But I knew the real reason.

The truth is that I'm not sure I love playing, I thought. *I worry I'm doing it only because I feel like I have to. Plus, the idea of this sport tearing me away from home just breaks my heart.*

Chapter Three

High School Star

Ursuline Academy is a private Catholic school in Wilmington, and beginning in sixth grade it educates only girls. It was where I went from seventh grade on.

The nice thing about all-girls schools is that there are no boys to compare yourself to. That may sound obvious and silly—I mean, *of course* there are no boys. It's an all-girls school! But that's not exactly what I mean. I'm talking about the fact that girls can really shine when boys aren't around. At Ursuline, pep rallies were for all of us. Our basketball squad was called the Raiders, not the "Lady Raiders." Playing sports at an all-girls school doesn't brand you as too tough or not girly enough. Instead you're powerful and respected. You're showing your friends and classmates that girls can be strong—and they don't need boys to tell them that.

You'd think that that kind of support system would have made me happy, right? But I wasn't. Playing better than ever—like when I led the Raiders to a state championship as an eighth grader—didn't either. I always left the court feeling totally empty.

I just couldn't figure out why I was training so much or playing so hard. By the time I was thirteen, I was traveling to out-of-town clinics or tournaments almost every weekend, sometimes sleeping in a hotel miles and miles away from my home and my sister. *She* was the person who needed me, not a bunch of basketball fans or college recruiters who wanted to snatch up the next high school star. Legendary Tennessee coach Pat Summitt flew to see one of my games early on in high school, then left that night, and while I was very honored to meet her, I wondered why her opinion of me mattered. *Impressing her is not why I was put on this earth,* I thought. I knew that if Lizzie wasn't even aware of all of my accomplishments on the court, then who was I playing for? Was I working like crazy for myself, or because I thought that it was what I was supposed to do?

I wasn't just burned out physically. My heart, mind, and soul were tired as well.

When I moved up to high school from eighth grade, my classes were in a different building. There were older kids in the new building, from freshman all the way up to seniors, and while I hadn't met a lot of them, they apparently knew who I was.

Early on in my freshman season, my teammates and I were walking through a narrow hallway on our way to the locker room so that we could get changed for an afternoon practice. I was toward the front of the group, followed right behind by our assistant coach, Peg Desendorf. As I made my way toward a mass of students just getting out of their last class, they turned, almost all together, and cleared a path for me. Some of them even reached out to touch my arm as I passed.

"What is going on, Coach Desendorf?" I asked as I turned to her.

"You were All-State as an eighth grader, Elena," she answered. "You're like a celebrity here."

I was humbled, but it wasn't enough to make me love basketball. In fact, I began to worry that if I let up even for a little bit, I'd be disappointing all my new fans.

I started playing harder than I ever had before. By the end of my freshman season, my team had a 25–1 record, and I was averaging twenty-eight points a game. We competed in—and won—the Diamond State Classic, a national girls' high school basketball tournament that was held in Wilmington and benefited the Special Olympics. This was especially meaningful to me because of Lizzie. Even though she wasn't able to participate in the Special Olympics, I'd seen some of her friends do it, and watching them receive medals made my heart sing.

In fact, remembering the Special Olympics was one of the few times I felt a sense of peace. I hated basketball, and that wouldn't change as I headed into my sophomore season, a year that put me on the national map more than ever.

Chapter Four

Free Throw Champion

In high school I became famous for my free throws.

The truth was, though, that I'd been great at them for years. When I was twelve, I was playing in an Amateur Athletic Union tournament, and we were down by two points as the clock ticked away. With one tenth of a second left in the game, I was fouled, sending me to the line for two shots. The whole game was up to me, and I was about to pass out from the pressure.

I thought about the thousands of free throws I'd made since I was little, and as the crowd began to roar, I visualized the ball going up, arcing forward, and then meeting the edge of the basket. When I unleashed the ball from my fingers, it did just that, moving through the net perfectly. We were down by one.

One shot, and we'll go into overtime, I told myself. With hundreds of eyes glued on me, I tried to shut out the noise in my head and shoot again.

Swoosh! The ball went through the basket, and regulation time ended. We entered extra time, then won the game. Later we went on to win the national title—something that wouldn't have happened if I hadn't made those two free throws.

That was a lot of pressure for someone who wasn't yet a teenager, right? While the stress of making free throws—especially when a game was on the line—didn't let off as the years went by, I luckily learned some skills that made the process easier. When I was in eighth grade, my varsity coach, Steve Johnson, taught me a surefire method for making a successful free throw.

"Three dribbles, then lift your arm into an L shape," he said. "Right after that, lift higher and flick the ball. Do this again and again, exactly the same way, and soon you'll be perfect."

I messed up a lot at first because it's not a very smooth free throw, but I stuck with the technique. Soon, every single time, I'd make the shot.

I quickly became one of the best free throw shooters in Delaware, and by the time my sophomore season rolled around, I was about to reach the top in the US, too.

In 2005 the national high school record for consecutive free throws made by a female player was seventy, and it had been set in 2002 by a girl from Indiana. When I was a sophomore, Ursuline was attending what every girls basketball team in the country considered to be the most important and elite basketball tournament all year: the Nike Tournament of Champions, which was always held in Phoenix.

I'd attended the Nike event the year before, but not under the circumstances I would in 2005. After all, the pressure on me had reached a boiling point, and not just because my coaches, teammates, and fans were depending on me to help us win the tournament. It was because I was just a few free throws away from breaking the national free throw record.

Get it over with, I told myself. *Then you won't feel so stressed anymore.*

As always, I was double- and triple-teamed throughout every single game. I was famous for making great shots from right near—and outside—the three-point line, so coaches for opposing teams never hesitated to send two, three, or even four of their biggest players to crowd around me. But when you're 6'5" and tower over the best high school basketball players in the country, your opponents know that guarding isn't enough. They understand that they can't just play defense. They had to commit fouls and hope for the best when I headed to the free throw line.

The problem was that I rarely—if ever—missed. And during the Nike tournament, when the best teams in the country were facing each other, it was no different.

We were playing a team we knew we would beat, but they were still putting up a great effort. As we neared the end of the half, I was fouled by one of my opponents, which sent me to the line for two shots. In most games when a player goes up for a free throw, fans of the opposing team will stand in the section facing the goal, wave their arms, yell, and whistle, in an attempt to distract the player. This time, however, the fans were almost silent. They knew what I knew: that if I scored both points, I'd officially break the high school free throw record.

I stepped up to the line and did just what I'd done ten

thousand times before. I closed my eyes, then opened them and looked down at the ball in my hands. I turned them up toward the basket. Three dribbles. L shape. Lift, and flick.

Swoosh. As the ball passed through the net, the crowd started to clap and cheer. "One more, Elena!" they screamed. Then they grew quiet once again.

My heart was pounding, and for a split second I was certain that my hands were going to get so sweaty that the ball would slip from them and roll away. *Just do what you've always done,* I told myself. *This is no big deal. Three dribbles. L shape. Lift, and flick.*

I watched the ball sail out of my hands, and then I closed my eyes. I wasn't even sure I wanted it to go in. Would breaking the record make me happier? Would it help me like basketball? Or was I trying to make history to please everyone else and because that's what I was supposed to do?

"Elena!" I heard my teammates scream my name as the crowd went wild. I opened my eyes and looked at the basket. The ball had passed through, and the net was just barely swinging. The ball bounced into a referee's hands, and my team surrounded me, hugging me tight.

I didn't feel like celebrating. I wasn't even happy. I just wanted to run home as fast as I could and sit quietly next to Lizzie, holding her hands and feeling a million miles away from the roar of the crowd.

Everyone had told me to expect the press to start calling after I broke the high school free throw record. And I knew without being told that college coaches would show up in droves at my games, then offer me scholarships. But I had no idea that at each game for the rest of my sophomore season I'd feel more and more pressure because everyone wanted to see my foul shot streak continue. No one—from my parents to my friends to the moms and dads who'd show up to cheer on an opposing team—wanted to see me miss.

My streak climbed through the seventies, all the way up to eighty. Making the shots felt so effortless, and I worried that if I missed, people would assume I'd been trying to. *I can't let them down,* I thought. *Everyone wants to see my record keep going higher.*

But it couldn't do that forever.

When I went to the line during one game late in my sophomore season to attempt my eighty-first consecutive free throw, I repeated every step I'd made—the exact same way—since my coach had first shown me how. Except, after this shot, the ball hit the rim and fell to the side. It landed in a mass of girls who were trying to rebound it, and I felt a strange sensation wash over me.

I'm relieved, I thought. *I'm actually relaxed because the pressure is off.*

For the first time in my life, making a mistake didn't seem to me like a character flaw or a terrible thing that had happened because I hadn't worked hard enough. Instead it gave me a break. It signaled that I was just as human as any other high school kid. And maybe, just maybe, I could make it one more day, week, or year before I finally burned out for good.

Chapter Five

Time Off

The end of my sophomore season was just as dramatic as the middle had been. In the state championship game against our biggest rival, St. Elizabeth High School—whom Ursuline had lost to in a devastating defeat earlier that year—I scored a record-high fifty points, leading my team to a 68–51 victory. Yep, you read that right. I scored fifty points, and the other team scored only one more point than that.

That year I averaged 28.5 points a game, and I maintained a 95 percent average for free throws.

How can I quit now, when I'm better than I've ever been? I thought. Leaving wasn't something I could seriously consider, especially because at the start of my junior year, Ursuline welcomed a new coach named Fran Burbidge, who came to us after coaching college teams throughout his entire career. He knew we had won three state championships, and I think he realized that coaching a team as good as Ursuline was a step up. With nationally ranked college coaches coming to see me play, he'd be in the national spotlight in a way he'd never been before.

As a junior, I trained and played as hard as I ever had,

yet my results were *almost* as good as they'd been during my sophomore year. Instead of averaging 28.5 points a game, I was at 28.3. And instead of making 95 percent of my free throws, I made 89 percent. Worst of all, the Raiders finished the year losing the state championship to St. Elizabeth, whom we'd stomped all over the year before. I was feeling like I might be at the end of my rope, but I couldn't give up. I just couldn't. People needed me.

In fact, crowds had started to show up at games and tournaments to get my autograph and have their photos taken with me. At one game against a team from Pennsylvania, we had to delay the start for twenty minutes so we could let in a line of people who wanted to see me. Oftentimes I'd have to stay forty-five minutes or more after games so I could greet fans and talk to the young girls and boys who wanted to get their pictures taken with me. If I gave it all up, wouldn't I be crushing their dreams too?

Finally, toward the end of my junior year, I decided it didn't matter.

If I don't take a break soon, I realized, *I'm going to burn out and give up basketball for good.*

The only looming issue was that I was almost positive I was going to be chosen for the USA Women's U19 World Cup Team, which was basically a fast track to the Olympics. I'd dreamed my whole life of competing in the Olympics, winning the gold, and standing with my hand over my heart while "The Star-Spangled Banner" played over the loudspeaker. I'd imagined tears running down my face, then pictured myself looking into the crowds to see my family crying too. If I said no to the U19 team, would I lose my shot at the Olympics forever? I decided to ask my dad for advice.

"Dad," I said, "I think I need a break. But if I put basketball on hold, will people forget I exist? Am I going to ruin my future?"

Dad was understanding but totally honest.

"Elena," he said, "I get it, but this could very well make USA Basketball not want to work with you ever again. So if you're serious that you feel this way—and I think you are—you need to go about it the right way. Call Carol Callan and talk with her."

Carol Callan was—and still is—the Women's National Team Director for USA Basketball, the governing body for men's and women's basketball. The idea of me—a teenager—ringing her up was like me calling the president, and I couldn't imagine that she'd give me the time of day. Much to my surprise, though, she did hear me out. She also understood where I was coming from.

"I'm shocked," she said at first. "But you have to be true to yourself. If you need rest, then that's the best step for your career. I'm just sorry you won't be competing with us."

I hated letting her, the team, and my country down, so it wasn't an easy choice to make. But I still decided I'd take the summer off. After the basketball season ended, I'd stop practicing and training after hours with John. I'd quit traveling to out-of-town tournaments on the weekends, and I'd politely decline to meet with recruiters and college coaches. Finally,

I'd make it clear to the media and my fans that I was stepping out of the spotlight, only for a little bit.

"I promise I'll be back next season," I told Fran and my other coaches, "but I just need to take this summer for myself."

That was only partially true. I also wanted to give the summer to Lizzie. Gene had gone to college—to Duke first, then to Middle Tennessee State University to play football as a tight end—and it was just me and Lizzie at home. My senior year would be my last with her, and I wanted to spend as much time with her as possible before I left home.

I also knew I'd become a role model to young girls and boys, and I wanted to show them that taking time away from the basketball court didn't mean I was going to be selfish. I wasn't just going to work on my tan all summer or party with my friends every night. I was going to volunteer at the Meadowood Program at Forest Oak Elementary School in Newark, Delaware, a place where Lizzie had spent a lot of time. I'd always believed that volunteering was important, and, in my mind, nobody needed time and attention more than Lizzie and people like her.

I worked with a woman named Connie Poultney, who had taught Lizzie for years, and I spent the summer taking the kids in the program on walks in the park. I taught them basic skills like writing or telling time, and I even broke my promise that I'd step away from basketball, when I shot hoops with them some afternoons. Most of these special children were kindergarten-aged, so they had no idea who I was on the court. But they all knew me as Lizzie's sister. And *that*, more than basketball stardom, was the best feeling in the world.

I'd always suspected I needed to find my mission in life outside of basketball, and that summer I think I did. I told my mom about it one day after coming home from Meadowood.

"When I go to college," I said, "I don't want it all to be about basketball."

"You shouldn't," Mom said. "There's a lot more to life than basketball. But what are you thinking of?"

I paused for a minute and got really serious. "I want to major in special education." Mom had taught special ed even before she'd had Lizzie, so she smiled right away. "This summer has shown me that I know how to connect with people with special needs. Too many people turn away from kids like Lizzie because they're scared, but I identify with them. I was born different just like them. I don't look like other people, and neither do they. I *get* them, Mom."

As the summer before my senior year in high school wrapped up, I felt more optimistic than I ever had in my life. I thought I'd screwed my head back on, and because of that, I assumed I could face basketball again.

I've got the rest of my life in front of me, I thought. *I've got basketball, a passion outside of it, my health, and a family I love. I'm not going to burn out, I just know it.*

Little did I know that the next year, in all respects, would be the most up-and-down of my whole life.

Chapter Six

Senior Year

When I stepped out onto the basketball court at the beginning of my senior year, I told myself I was ready. This season Ursuline would reclaim the state championship title. This year I'd decide which college scholarship to take. And this year I'd find my passion for the sport again. After all, if I'd taken the summer off and *still* decided to lace up my shoes and pick up a ball when the summer was over, didn't that mean I'd liked playing at least a little bit?

Almost immediately I realized I'd been deceiving myself. I thought, *The truth is I just missed my teammates. I came back because I don't want to let them down.*

Because of that, I forged ahead. I started training again with John, and I practiced one-on-one with my dad and anyone else who would play with me. Fran and I discussed a workout schedule in preparation for the season, which would start in the late fall, and I began to carefully consider my college options with my parents. I was leaning toward the University of Connecticut, which had the best team in the country, but I also liked the University of Tennessee, whose legendary coach, Pat Summitt, had been so kind to me when she'd watched one of my games the year before. Villanova and Middle Tennessee State University were also at the top of my list. Duke had offered me a scholarship, as had UNC years before, but I'd decided not to go to either of them.

That fall I encountered a situation I hadn't been expecting.

I was leaving class one day, heading toward my locker to pack up my stuff and go home, when the captain of the varsity volleyball team approached me.

"Have you ever played volleyball?" she asked.

I had to think for a little bit. "Um, I think I did at camp. And when we go to the beach in the summer, sometimes I play there. Why?"

"Because we have an injured player," she said. "She can't play in the next game, and we thought maybe you could fill in for her near the net because you're so tall."

I'd never even considered playing volleyball. I was all about basketball, all the time, and a big part of me worried that if I focused on anything else—even for one game—I might fall out of my groove.

I decided to talk to Fran about it, and he wasn't concerned. As long as I dedicated myself to basketball when practices started, he didn't see how someone who worked as hard as I did would suffer for trying something new.

I played one volleyball game, and I loved it. In fact, I enjoyed it so much that I went back for one more game, then another. During practice I never felt pressured to be the best, and during games I never worried that the whole team was depending on me alone.

For the first time in forever, I thought, *I'm having fun.*

I was enjoying volleyball in a pure way, untainted by stress or fear of letting anyone down. I just liked the way it made my body feel. My heart soared when I spiked the ball or tapped it lightly to a teammate, who'd then knock it over the net. There was a simplicity to volleyball that didn't happen on the basketball court—less running back and forth, more immediate gratification, and shots that happened in quicker succession. The game moved so quickly that I didn't have time to do anything but focus on getting the ball over the net, away from the ground, or to a teammate.

Plus, volleyball didn't have any of the baggage that basketball did. I could be anyone I wanted to be on the volleyball court. There were no looming scholarship offers, no Olympic dreams, and no state championship title to bring back home.

Even though I was a total newbie, I was a great player. By the end of the season, our team was almost undefeated, and much to everyone's surprise, I helped lead them to the state championships. Like the varsity basketball team, we were hoping to avenge a loss from the previous year, when we'd been defending our title.

The pressure I felt before the final game was so different from what I felt playing basketball, though. If we won the title, I'd be thrilled, but if we lost, I wouldn't feel crushed. I'd just know we'd played our hardest, and a loss wouldn't be a personal failure.

During the championship, I played with more heart than I ever had in my life—and had more fun doing it. I had sixteen kills and six blocks, and Ursuline won! We finished the season with a 22–2 record.

Unfortunately, the high I was feeling about volleyball quickly ended when basketball season went into full swing. It wasn't just because I was training so hard, though. It was because I'd formally accepted a scholarship from the UConn Huskies. I'd be going to Storrs, Connecticut, for college, playing on the best women's college team in the nation, and I realized I was about to throw myself 150 percent into a future I wasn't sure I wanted. I was faking my commitment, even when I signed on the dotted line. But how could I have said no? Someone as good as Elena Delle Donne was expected to go all the way, and that started at a place like UConn.

My heart was suffering, and my health was too. Starting just after Thanksgiving, I'd suddenly begun moving more slowly than I usually did during practice. When I woke up in the mornings, I couldn't go running, but it was because I wasn't physically able to get out of bed, not because I wanted to sleep in. I'd begun dozing off in class, I ran a low-grade fever for days, and I had aches and pains all over my body on and off all day.

When I went to the doctor, I assumed he'd diagnose me with the flu. Instead he took a few tests and told me I had mono.

"You'll need to take a few weeks' rest to recover," he said. "So no basketball until this thing is gone."

My team was set to attend the Nike Tournament of Champions in Phoenix—where I'd broken the girls' high school free throw record two years before—and I'd be forced to sit on the sidelines. But was I disappointed? I wasn't. I felt a little guilty, but I was looking forward to the rest. There would be no pressure to be the best, no stress that I'd have to save the game, and no days and weeks of mentally and physically preparing myself to play against the most difficult teams in the country.

I hope you don't think I was abandoning my teammates emotionally. I wasn't. I wanted badly for them to win, but I didn't want it to be all because of me.

I feel awful for being so selfish, I thought. *But the doctor told me that my liver is having trouble and my spleen is enlarged. Right now I just need to think about me.*

When we lost every game in the tournament, though, I felt terrible. I beat myself up for not being able to play, and I hated myself for feeling even the tiniest bit of relief at getting to rest.

For the rest of the season, I decided, *I'm not going to think about myself. I'm going to play harder than I ever have, because everyone is depending on me.*

We won almost all of the rest of the season's games—including having a fifteen-game winning streak—and I was on the floor for all of them. We won the state championship, I was named the top female college recruit in the nation, I played in the Women's Basketball Coaches Association (WBCA) high school All-America game, and I was the first and only student ever to score more than two thousand points for Ursuline. Throughout every single one of those wins and honors, I forged ahead, thinking only about basketball, forcing myself to believe—with every bone in my body—that basketball was what I was put on this earth to do.

After all, when I played it, everyone won—except for me.

Chapter Seven

Burnout

When I graduated from Ursuline as the most decorated and celebrated student athlete in the school's history, my entire family wasn't there to see it. Gene didn't come home from MTSU, and Lizzie wasn't in the stands clapping for me.

Why? Because *I* didn't even attend my graduation. While my fellow classmates were shaking our headmaster's hand and claiming their diplomas, I was on my way up to UConn, where I'd be starting summer classes and training with the women's basketball team.

Most of my family still lives in Delaware, and leaving them broke my heart. My dad had done well as a real estate developer, so at that point he and Mom had just purchased a house and some property outside of Wilmington. It was thirty-five acres, and Dad had brought home a golf cart for Lizzie to ride in. (And she *loved* it!) There was nothing I liked more than walking or riding with her outside when the weather was nice, letting her feel the wind blow across her face and through her hair. Wind and the warmth of the sun were two of the things that put Lizzie most at ease, giving her a connection to the outside world that most people take for granted. Because I had moved to Connecticut, I wouldn't be able to see that smile on her face when she was outside, except during school breaks and family vacations. I wouldn't get to feel her squeeze my hand, signaling she was happy.

Instead of being home, celebrating the end of high school with my friends and family, I was walking away from a pickup game on my first night at UConn, and I was certain I never wanted to play basketball again.

The morning after that initial scrimmage, I woke up early to get ready for my first class. It was an English class, and the teacher couldn't have been nicer. She gave us an overview of what the summer semester would be like, and she handed us a syllabus and outline for our assignments, explaining that we'd have a paper due in two weeks. Then she began discussing the material that would be on our first exam.

I lifted a pencil to take notes, then put it down.

What's the point of remembering any of this if I won't be here for the next class?

I'd made up my mind. I was going to leave UConn that night.

On my way back to my dorm room, I pulled my cell phone out of my pocket and called a friend who I'll refer to as Pam.

"Pam," I said. "I need to go home. Can you pick me up?"

"What's wrong?" she asked. "Is everything okay?"

I started to cry. "I just need to go home. I need to see my family. Please come get me."

The great thing about Pam was that she knew that if I said

something as serious as I just had, I usually meant it—and there was no time to ask questions.

"I'll be there whenever you need me," she said.

I told Pam not to come until after midnight because I didn't want anyone to know I was leaving. My roommate was on the basketball team too, and if I'd told her I was going home, she'd have thought I was crazy. *No one*—especially the top high school recruit in the country—walked away from a full ride at UConn, even for a day. I fully expected people to think I was insulting Geno and the whole program he'd built. I was ashamed, and I couldn't bear to hear my roommate question me, or even try to persuade me to stay. I just wanted to get out of the state of Connecticut as quickly as possible and not answer any questions till I had my head on straight again. I wanted to get home to my parents, then explain myself later.

After my roommate fell asleep, I quietly packed a bag. I figured I could just come back later and claim my larger items; right now all I needed were some clothes, my toiletries, and my computer. I'd even leave my basketball shoes in the closet. Why would I need them? I had no plans to wear them again soon—if ever.

Just after midnight my cell phone vibrated. When I answered, Pam told me she was waiting outside in a parking lot. I grabbed my bag, took a deep breath, and looked around my dorm room.

I might be making a huge mistake by leaving, I thought, *but if I stay, it'll be the biggest mistake of my life.*

Pam knew not to ask too many questions on the way home. She didn't have to, though; I explained everything.

"When the team captain said that the most important thing we could give to the team was passion, I made my decision. I can't lie to her or someone as important as Coach Auriemma. I can't play on the best team in the country and hate what I'm doing. I can work harder than everyone else, but if I'm miserable, I'll fail. And the whole team will lose with me."

"Have you felt this way for a while?" Pam asked.

"Since I was thirteen," I said. "I've just been hoping it would go away."

The drive from Storrs to Wilmington was almost five hours, and Pam didn't stop the whole time. She knew I was desperate to get home, so she drove like crazy, even when I nodded off and fell into a deep sleep. I think every muscle in my body was more tired than it had ever been in my life.

We pulled up to the front of my house just as the sun was coming up.

"Pam, I can't thank you enough," I said as I woke up.

"I love you, Elena," she responded. "And you're doing the right thing. Call me later."

As she pulled out of the driveway, I felt my chest tighten. Even as I'd packed my bag, and even as I'd let my feelings of guilt and shame pour from my mouth on the drive with Pam, I hadn't let myself cry. I'd decided I had to be strong. I had to keep moving until I decided what I wanted to do next. I had to keep myself from falling apart more than I already had.

I walked to my parents' front door and rang the doorbell,

since I didn't have a key. When it opened, my mom was standing there in her bathrobe.

"Elena? What are you doing home?" She looked shocked.

I dropped my bag, ran into her arms, and broke down in tears.

PART TWO
REBOUND

Chapter Eight

The Hardest Summer of My Life

"Crazy."

"Spoiled little rich girl."

"Ungrateful."

Those were just a few of the things people wrote or said about me the summer after I left UConn. And those were some of the nicer words.

My parents even had a hard time being understanding.

"Basketball has been your dream since you were four," my dad said. "Now you're throwing it all away?" He had a developer's brain, and he'd spent his life weighing decisions, making calculations, and building foundations. Tearing them down felt *huge* to him.

"Are you sure you're just burned out? It's not something else?" Mom added. "Maybe you're just not feeling well?"

"I'm *not* feeling well," I said. "Basketball is literally making me sick."

Eventually, Mom and Dad came around and realized how serious I was, but those first few weeks weren't easy. They— and everyone else I'd grown up with—didn't understand how someone as talented as I was, who'd worked toward a scholarship to a school as prestigious as UConn for so many years, could just walk away from it. They were terrified I'd regret my decision. Sure, some people, especially college kids who'd spent their high school years exhausted from too much homework and too many activities, sympathized with me, but others were horrified. After all, I'd been given something that most people can only dream of, yet I'd thrown it away.

To be honest, sometimes *I* wasn't even sure why I'd left UConn. Sure, I was tired and lost, but was that reason enough? I'd been born with a God-given talent, so wasn't I supposed to do something with that? But then I would remember how I felt when I first saw Lizzie after I got home from UConn, when I walked through my parents' front door and went into her bedroom.

"Hi, Lizzie," I said to her, even though I knew she couldn't hear me. Suddenly she perked up, her eyes opening. *She can smell me,* I realized. Then I leaned down to her bed, lifted her up very slightly, and hugged her. Even though I could feel the bones in her frail back, she reached her arms around me and squeezed me tighter than she'd ever held me before.

Does she know I'm not leaving again? I wondered, immediately realizing it was true. Lizzie had always been able to communicate with me through different kinds of touches, taps, and hugs, and I knew that a squeeze as tight as the one she'd just given me signaled that she knew I was home. For good.

So Lizzie's the real reason I came home, I realized right then. *I'm just not going to be happy if I'm away from her. I can't Skype her or text her, so this—and nothing else—is what we both need.*

The question remained, however, what I was going to do next. I'd spent so long doing what I assumed other people thought I should, that I knew I was going to have trouble making any kind of decision. So I figured I'd take it one day at a time. I'd go with my heart. And I'd make any next steps mine and mine alone.

At about eleven a.m., just a few hours later, my cell phone rang. I looked down at the caller ID, and my heart stopped. It was a Connecticut number, and I knew it had to be Coach Auriemma.

"H-h-hello?" I answered after three rings, my voice cracking.

"Hi, Elena. It's Geno Auriemma." His voice was measured but kind. He didn't sound angry, just a little bit concerned. "You didn't show up at morning practice, and your roommate said you weren't there and hadn't left a note. Is everything okay?"

I hesitated. "Umm. Well, I'm sorry. I'm so sorry." I could feel tears forming in the corner of my eyes, and I started to worry that I was going to break down again. Just then my mom walked into the room, and she sat on the couch next to me, then held my hand.

"Sorry for what?" he asked. "Whatever it is, just tell me. It's okay."

I suddenly realized I wasn't going to be able to hold it together, so I handed the phone to my mom, who introduced herself and started talking.

"Coach," she said, "we're so sorry, but Elena needs to be home right now. She's not sure what she wants to do. She—and all of us—are so grateful for the scholarship and for everything you've done, but she can't play right now. It's too much for her."

"Has anything happened? Is she hurt or sick?" he asked.

"No," Mom said, "but she just doesn't feel she can play basketball now."

I could hear silence on the other end of the line, and I hoped and prayed Coach Auriemma wasn't angry. I knew he was probably shocked and terribly disappointed, but I didn't want him to hate me. Instead he was just as calm and kind as he'd always been when he began speaking.

"Mrs. Delle Donne, I've seen this before. Homesickness is completely understandable. So are nerves. But Elena is one of the most all-around skilled players I've seen in my career, and I'd hate for her talent to go to waste this summer. Even for a day." He paused. "That's why I encourage you to drive her back to Storrs as soon as possible."

My mom has always been able to read my body language better than anyone else. I always thought it was because of Lizzie. After all, when you have a child who can communicate only through touch and expressions, you begin to pick up subtle physical clues from them. At that moment, I'm positive that despair was written all over my face. With my arms crossed and my shoulders slumped, I'm sure I looked about as ready to drive back to Storrs as I was to drive to my own funeral.

"Coach," Mom said, clearing her throat. "I know my

daughter. I'm looking at her right now. She has never given up on anything in her life before, but I think this time is different. Unfortunately, I won't be driving her back to Storrs. But we will be in touch soon."

When Mom hung up the phone, I laid my head down on the table and started sobbing all over again.

Part of the reason why a coach like Geno Auriemma gets as far as he does is because he doesn't give up. When UConn kept losing during his first season as head coach, he knew he could turn the team around, so he kept pushing them, telling his players they'd win the national title someday. Sure enough, they did, going from 4–12 his first season as coach to national champions in ten years.

All that summer Coach Auriemma checked in with me every now and then.

"We're holding your scholarship till August," he'd say. "And your place on the team, of course. We miss you."

But my heart was telling me to stay home. Home was safe. Home didn't pressure me. Home didn't think I should play basketball just because I was so talented at it.

That summer my family rented a house in Stone Harbor, a town on one of the southernmost barrier islands on the Jersey Shore. I loved spending time on the beach, jumping in the waves, and standing in line for Springer's super-delicious ice cream. We planned to vacation there for a few weeks, and I couldn't think of a better place to unwind and forget about making a decision about my future.

The only issue was that Coach Auriemma had a house in Avalon, the town north of Stone Harbor. His house was just a few blocks from my family's rental, and he was going to be there the same time we were. I mean, what were the chances?

It would be embarrassing and childish to avoid someone who'd been so patient and kind to me, so I called him before our vacation began and made a plan to visit him one day for lunch. *No pressure,* I told myself. *You're just there to talk.*

On a blazing hot summer afternoon in July, I put on a pair of jeans and a nice shirt, hopped on my bike, and rode up the island's main thoroughfare toward Coach Auriemma's house. I passed candy and fudge shops, stores selling shells and souvenirs, and kids walking with their families toward the beach. As I steered my bike into the street where his house was situated, I took a deep breath. I wasn't sure what he was going to ask me, and I had no idea what I was planning to say, but I promised myself I'd be levelheaded and straightforward about it.

Coach Auriemma's wife, Kathy, greeted me at the door.

"Hi, Elena. It's so nice to see you. Come on inside."

I walked into their spacious, comfortable house, decorated with bright colors and family photos, and saw Coach Auriemma sitting in an easy chair. He rose to greet me, then pulled me into a hug.

"I hope you're having a good summer," he said.

"I am," I said, "and it's good to see you."

As Kathy put a few sandwiches on plates and made lemonade in the kitchen, Coach and I talked for what felt like hours. I asked him about the team and practices, and he asked me about my family. He told me about his plans for the upcoming basketball season, and I apologized for putting him in such an awkward situation with the athletic department and the UConn administration. He told me not to worry, that he'd talked to school officials, and they had a great idea.

"I know you're not interested in basketball anymore, so you can keep your scholarship and come back to school—yet skip the season."

My jaw tightened as I struggled to answer. "Coach, it's not just basketball," I practically whispered. "It's so much more than that. I just can't come back."

"We won't expect you to practice or even go to games. We'll leave you alone. The university just wants you to attend, no strings attached."

I looked down and clasped my hands between my legs. I hated saying what I was about to, but I couldn't lie to him. Not again.

"No. I can't. Thank you for being so understanding, but I can't go back."

He kept on. "I know it's hard. Believe me. I can't tell you how many students I've picked up off the floor year after year after year. But we don't want to lose you. We—"

Just then I saw Kathy emerge from the kitchen holding a pitcher of lemonade. She had a look on her face that was all business.

"Geno," she said. "Stop. She's not going back to UConn. Leave her alone."

Coach Auriemma and I sat in stunned silence for a minute.

When I finally looked up, I could see the expression on his face, and it was the last thing I'd ever expected.

He's sad, I thought. *Not angry and not shocked. He's just sad.*

But there was nothing I could do. Finally, after so many years and so much blood, sweat, and tears, I'd promised to look out for myself.

The problem was, though, that I didn't really know what I wanted to do after the summer ended. Sure, I'd decided I wasn't going back to UConn, but where would I go instead? And what would I do? Should I take more time off? And if I wasn't going to play basketball, then how would I spend all the hours I'd have on my hands?

When we got back from the beach, I started taking a lot of long walks. Like I said, my parents' house was spread across thirty-five acres, and there were few things I liked more than to wake up early in the morning and head out into the woods. My beloved Great Dane, Champ, had died three days after I'd come home from Connecticut, and it broke my heart not to be with him. Even though every step reminded me of him, I was starting to manage. On those beautiful, long walks, I wasn't worrying about what was next. I was just trying to enjoy myself.

Be in the moment, I told myself. *Because in the moment there's no pressure.*

One morning just after dawn, I was navigating my way through some tall trees, watching the sunlight peek between the green leaves that almost entirely covered the sky. As I looked up, a ray broke through and made me squint. Suddenly a thought hit me.

I'll go to school nearby, at the University of Delaware. I'm not going to play basketball either. I'm going to join the volleyball team and have fun playing a sport I really, truly love. A sport that's actually fun, with no expectations.

I almost jumped for joy, realizing that I knew what I was going to do for the next four years. I was going to live and play on my own terms rather than because I thought it was what people wanted me to do. I was going to choose my own path rather than the one that was expected of me. And I'd be close to Lizzie. I could see her every day if I wanted to!

I started to jog back toward my house. Then I stopped suddenly, feeling nauseated.

I'm fine. I was probably just looking at the sun too long. Or maybe I'm still just tired.

I had no idea how very wrong I was. Those blissful walks in the woods that summer had already changed my life forever.

Chapter Nine

Lyme Disease

A few days after that first bout of nausea, I started to feel sick in a way I never had before.

"Mom," I said one morning when I stumbled into the kitchen for breakfast, "I feel like I have the flu. I'm exhausted, and my joints are killing me, but I don't have a fever. This is weird."

Mom took my temperature, and sure enough, it came in right at 98.6. Perfectly normal.

"Let's keep an eye on things," she said. "Maybe you're just worn out, so get some rest, and if it gets worse, we'll go to the doctor."

I stayed inside all day, barely ate anything, crawled into bed early that night, and woke up at dawn with the worst pain I've felt in my life. The achiness wasn't just in my joints, though; my head was throbbing on one side, and the light that was starting to pour in through my bedroom blinds made me feel like I was going to throw up. But instead of running to the bathroom, all I could manage to do was lie still, breathing as slowly and steadily as I could so that I could keep the nausea at bay. As my head throbbed, I drifted into a fitful sleep, and about an hour or so later my mom peeked her head in the door.

"Elena," she asked, "are you up?"

I couldn't even lift my head up as I squinted at her and started talking. "I feel awful. I think I have a migraine. Can we go to the doctor?"

"Of course," she said, "You should try to eat something first, though. I'll call the doctor, and we'll go see him after we drop Lizzie off."

Mom had fixed a beautiful breakfast, like she always did, but I couldn't even look at it. While she made me an emergency appointment and helped Lizzie into the car, I walked to the couch, lay down, and closed my eyes. I waited for her in silence. Then she came back, led me out the door, and seated me inside the car with Lizzie. After we left Lizzie at school, we pulled into the doctor's office parking lot, and I felt like it took me ten minutes to make it into the building.

"What's going on?" the doctor asked as I was sitting on the exam table.

I spelled out the whole list of strange symptoms I was having. He took my temperature, checked my pulse, looked inside my throat, felt the glands in my neck, and did all the normal things that doctors usually do when they're trying to figure out what's wrong with their patient. Then he looked at me, seriously, and started talking again.

"I can't really see anything that's unusual. You don't have a temperature, so it doesn't appear to be an infection. Have you come into contact with anyone who's been sick lately? Or has anything else happened?"

I thought for a minute. "Um, nothing much. I've been with my family since I left UConn, so I haven't seen that many people. I've been taking lots of walks in the woods mostly. I've just been so stressed out, so I'm trying to take it easy."

My doctor paused for a second in concentration. "Have you noticed any strange marks on your skin?" he asked.

"Nothing," I answered. "Why?"

"No reason. Let's run some tests. I don't think this is the flu or mono, so I want to rule out anything that's more serious."

I went home and straight back to bed. A day or so later my doctor called and told me that the results had come back.

"You tested positive for Lyme disease," he said. "You need to start taking antibiotics immediately."

Those of you who live in the suburbs or the country, where there are lots of deer around, might have heard of Lyme disease. A lot of people who spend most of their time in cities haven't. Even though I lived with woods all around me, though, it wasn't something anyone I knew had come down with. Maybe I'd heard about Lyme disease on the news, or from a friend of a friend, but it had never affected my life directly.

That all changed in the summer of 2008.

Lyme disease is a bacterial infection that's carried by deer ticks. Even though I'd never found a tick on me, I must have been bitten by one at some point during one of my walks, and it then transmitted the disease into my body. Usually a tick has to be attached to you for a day or two for the infection to begin. In my case, I have no idea how long I'd had the tick, but it was definitely enough time for me to get sick.

The clearest sign that someone has Lyme disease is a bull's-eye rash at the site of the bite. Literally it looks like someone tattooed a bull's-eye right on your skin. I didn't have that, so it's a good thing my doctor had decided to run tests. Otherwise he might have misdiagnosed me with the flu or mono, which is what happens to a lot of people. Those people then don't get the medication they need fast enough, and the infection spreads. They start to feel worse, and as the bacteria stays in their body, their joint pain, stiffness, migraines, or exhaustion lasts longer. They may even suffer nerve damage that affects them for the rest of their lives.

Luckily, I wasn't one of those people—or so I thought at first. I took the antibiotics my doctor prescribed for almost three weeks, and I felt better immediately. My migraines went away, my body stopped aching, and soon I was ready to face my first day as a freshman at the University of Delaware.

If there was anything the University of Delaware was known for, it wasn't basketball, but that was just fine with me. Campus was in a town called Newark, which was only thirty minutes from my parents and Lizzie, but it was light-years away from my burnout. I knew it would be the perfect place to start a new chapter of my life.

I could have lived at home if I'd wanted to, but I decided to move into a dorm, like what I thought a normal college student would do. I dreamed of being a regular girl for the next four years, with no six a.m. training sessions, no weekends away booked months in advance, and nothing to worry about except where to study or what club to join. All I wanted was to blend right in with everyone else.

Who was I kidding? I was pretty much the most famous person on campus from day one. Random strangers would give me sympathetic looks on the way to class, and I could see people whispering when I walked outside my dorm. I knew I was easy to spot because I was the tallest girl in the whole school, but it still made me sad. People thought I'd dropped out of UConn because I was pregnant, on drugs, or had had some kind of massive mental breakdown, and I wished more than anything else that they'd just forget me and move on.

I knew I couldn't control what anyone thought of me, so I chose to just shrug it off. *I guess being the juiciest gossip in the dining hall is better than being miserable twenty-four hours a day,* I reassured myself.

I still loved school from moment one. UD was welcoming and comfortable, full of people who loved the state of Delaware just as much as I did. My mom had gone there, so it felt like a part of my history—a legacy that I could grow into—and maybe I could become as wonderful and accomplished as my mom. I saw familiar faces from preschool, high school, YMCA youth league, and more. I could go home on the weekends to do my laundry and have dinner with my family, and if I was missing Lizzie, I could hop into my car and be by her side in no time at all. I was living day to day for myself, making no big plans for the future, and for the first time in ages, I was actually feeling relaxed.

But sports are a huge part of who I am, and, luckily, I'd realized that the moment I'd decided to go to Delaware. At the end of the summer, I'd asked UConn to release me from my scholarship so I could play varsity sports at another school, and they'd agreed. On the morning that the women's volley-ball team opened up their roster to walk-ons, I was the first person in line to try out.

I made the team. I was officially a fighting Blue Hen!

Chapter Ten

Volleyball

Even though the University of Delaware women's volleyball team didn't exactly draw big crowds—there were maybe 750 fans at our home opener—the team was nothing to laugh at. They'd finished the 2007 season with a 31–5 record, had won the Colonial Athletic Association (CAA) title, and had made it to the NCAA women's volleyball tournament for the first time in their history. They'd won in the first round, in fact. Coach Bonnie Kenny had been with the team for seven seasons, and she was building up a great program, with enthusiastic players, proven results, and a togetherness the likes of which I hadn't encountered in years. Plus, when I found out that I'd made the team, she greeted me like I was a part of her family, calling my parents to see if there was anything special she or her staff could do for me. Knowing I'd probably get a hundred calls from the media, Coach Kenny held a press conference for me so that I could speak for myself, on my own terms. I was smiling from ear to ear as I answered reporters' questions.

Once volleyball season started, I'd be competing for a spot

as a middle hitter. Having to vie for a position was totally new to me because I'd always been a starter on every team—in every sport. But even if I had to warm the bench for a few games, I didn't care. I was having fun! There was no pressure to be the best person on the team. On the basketball court, I'd been so good—and so tough on myself—that I'd made each practice and game a battle of me versus me. That didn't happen with volleyball. All that mattered was that I played hard *with* my team.

I also knew I wasn't expected to hold the whole team together. When I was called off the bench, my job was to be on the front line and never leave it. In basketball I'd been the offense, defense, rebounder, lead field goal shooter, and star of the three-point shot. In volleyball I could play one position really well, and that would help my team—all of us together—win matches.

And win we did.

We finished the season 19–16, captured the CAA championship for a second straight year, and received our second NCAA tournament bid.

I can't believe I'm at the NCAA tournament for volleyball rather than basketball, I remember thinking. *Never in a million years would I have expected that!* But was I full of regret, dreaming longingly of basketball glory? Not at all. When I look at photos of myself during that tournament, I see that I have the biggest smile on my face because I was having a blast. We were the underdogs, not expected to advance to the second round. When we lost in the first round, we accepted it.

We weren't disappointed, because we'd had a brilliant season.

For the first time in my whole life, no one said anything to me about basketball either. When I went home on Sundays for dinner, my parents steered clear of the subject. My classmates were so excited about the volleyball team doing well that they talked to me about volleyball, not basketball.

Even the UD women's basketball head coach, Tina Martin, gave me a comfortable distance. She never called me, and she told her assistant coaches not to either. Once, I passed her in a hall near the gym, and all she did was nod and politely say, "Hello." I ran into varsity basketball players every now and then, but they talked to me about classes or my volleyball matches, never about basketball. I later found out that Coach Martin had given them instructions to avoid the subject of basketball completely with me.

I kept thinking about something that had happened to me during the summer, though. One day after I'd returned home from Storrs, when I was forcing any thoughts about basketball out of my mind, I'd decided to pick Lizzie up at the Mary Campbell Center. I knew most of Lizzie's classmates and teachers, and as I left my car and walked toward the center's entrance, I was approached by a woman with a familiar face. It was a woman in a wheelchair named Dawn, who had cerebral palsy just like Lizzie.

"Elena?" she asked tentatively.

"Oh, hi, Dawn!" I said to reassure her. We'd only spoken a few times, but there was no reason for her to be shy.

"I just wanted to say that I'm a huge basketball fan."

I tried not to, but I couldn't help cringing inside. I hated the thought of disappointing anyone—especially Dawn.

Luckily, being upset with me was the last thing on her mind, which I discovered when she kept talking.

"I know you're not playing anymore, but I just want you to know how much I still look up to you. And I hope you didn't quit because you think you're not good enough. You are, and you should do everything you can with your abilities, just like we do."

I was stunned. *So not only is she* not *disappointed in me,* I thought, *but she's worried that I'm disappointed in myself!*

The honest truth was that I wasn't frustrated with my decision, but part of what Dawn said still nagged at me. She respected me as a basketball player, not a volleyball player. I knew volleyball was fun, but it wasn't totally fulfilling me. It wasn't *me.*

When young girls had approached me after volleyball games or out in public and asked for autographs, I'd always signed them *Elena Delle Donne, #11.* That was my basketball number, not my volleyball number! I wasn't sure if I did that because that was how I was known to the world, or because that was how I saw myself.

All I knew was that there were so many things I really missed about basketball. I loved how much it challenged me physically and mentally, and how it kept me on my toes— constantly. I just wasn't someone who needed to kick back all the time. Sure, I knew I had to have fun in my life, but wasn't there room for something that would really push me forward?

I can't believe it, I said to myself, *but I want to think about playing basketball again.* Then the strangest thought hit me. *Maybe I'm not as burned out as I thought?*

It took me a long time to realize it, but one of the amazing things about burning out is that it doesn't have to signal the end of something—even though you might think that when you're totally falling apart. Feeling drop-dead exhausted or hating even the slightest thought of something might just mean that you need to break up with it, then get back together when the time's right. Sure, I'd taken a little vacation from playing the summer after my junior year of high school, but maybe that hadn't been enough? Maybe, as the saying goes, true love is meant to be if you say good-bye to something, and then it comes back to you?

I wasn't ready to make a decision just yet, so I gave myself some time to think about it.

UD isn't a huge sports school, so a lot of the varsity athletes ran in the same circles, and many of them were my friends. I'd grown close to a basketball player named Meghan McLean, and one night during the winter of my freshman year, I approached her.

"Meghan?" I asked with just the tiniest bit of hesitation. "Do you want to shoot some hoops tonight?"

I suppose I shouldn't have been surprised by her reaction, but I was. She looked at me with her mouth wide open, then didn't say a word.

"I mean, I'm not making any commitments," I continued, "but I miss being on the court. I think. I just want to see what it feels like to get some shots up with someone."

Meghan finally nodded her head, and that night we met at the Bob Carpenter Center, the five-thousand-seat arena on campus. "The Bob," as everyone calls it, is home to the volleyball and basketball teams, so I'd been there a million times. Someone used to the huge ten-thousand-seat stadiums at Duke or UConn might have joked that the Bob looked more like a high school stadium than something you'd find at a state university, but I always thought it was perfectly cozy. It wasn't grand and intimidating. When I played at the Bob, I felt close to the crowd, like I was watching them as much as they were watching me.

As Meghan fumbled in her gym bag that night, trying to find the keys to the arena, I felt the strangest sensation wash over me. *I'm actually nervous about playing basketball,* I thought. *I've played for so long that I could make a basket in my sleep, but right now I feel like I'm about to go on a first date.*

As Meghan and I shot and rebounded for about an hour, I realized I was happy in a way I hadn't been in years. My head was clear, and I wasn't overthinking anything. I was just *feeling*, and the sensation was pure bliss.

I love this sport, I realized, *and I think I'm going to play it here at Delaware.*

Chapter Eleven

Basketball, Take Two

I didn't decide to join the Blue Hen basketball team right away, nor did I rush into my volleyball coach's office and tell her I wasn't coming back for a second season. I wanted to let the thought of going back sink in, and, of course, I had to talk it over with my family.

When I told my dad, he wasn't surprised at all. He was also over-the-moon excited because he could sense how eager I was.

"I know you, Elena," he said. "I watched you pick up a basketball for the first time when you were four, and I've never seen anyone so attached to anything. I've always known basketball is a part of you as much as your nose is to your face." Then he paused and looked at me seriously. "When you decide to start playing again—*if* you decide to play again—just remember the feeling you have now, which is love. You love this game. Don't let all the other stuff get to you."

Dad understood my feelings about basketball better than anyone else, and right at that moment his words really hit me. This time around—if I actually decided to go back—I wasn't going to play basketball because of what other people wanted. I wasn't going to be on a team because it was the only path in front of me. Now that I'd cleared out all the noise in my head and realized that I actually *did* love the game, I was going to play for me. Going back would be my decision—and mine alone—and I would head into it with one purpose: to feel good.

When I met with Coach Martin a few weeks later, I still hadn't made up my mind for sure. I was leaning toward playing again, but I knew it was a huge—possibly life-changing—decision, so I really just wanted to give her a heads-up that I was thinking about it. I wanted to ease into the conversation, so for forty-five minutes we talked about everything but basketball. Then I broke the ice.

"Coach," I said, "I think I might play basketball again. But I'm really not sure. A part of me never wants to start in another game. But if I decide to, I'll be in touch, because you've been so great to me this year. Thank you for that."

Just like she'd been all year, Coach Martin didn't crowd me or pressure me. In fact, she didn't give a single hint that what I was saying might change her whole program. Instead all she said was, "You're welcome. It was so nice to see you today. I really enjoyed all that we talked about."

I'm sure Coach Martin saw my face in the stands of the Bob over the next few months. I snuck into a few games to see the dynamics of the team. *I like everything about them,* I thought when I watched them. *They look like they're having a great time together.*

Early that spring I still wasn't ready to make a decision, but I started working out with John Noonan again. My body fell into the familiar groove it had known since I was four, and playing began to feel natural again—like it was a gift, not a burden. By May I'd made up my mind, and I called Coach Martin to tell her the news.

"Coach," I said proudly, "I'd like to play for Delaware. That's if you'll have me, of course."

I couldn't see her face break out into a smile, but I could hear her laugh on the other end of the line as she started to talk.

"Elena, nothing would make me happier. But it's not about me. It's about you. So know that I and every single person on our team wants you to enjoy yourself next year."

I think I will, I told myself. *I've got a few months to get ready, so right now just feel good about the decision I've made.*

The Blue Hens women's basketball team wasn't exactly a basketball powerhouse. Not like UConn, at least. They'd finished the previous season with a 15–15 record, they had been to the NCAA tournament only twice—once during the 2007–08 season, when they'd lost in the first round—and if they were lucky, they got maybe a thousand fans per game. That's one fifth of the Bob Carpenter Center capacity.

When I joined the team during the 2009–10 season as a redshirt freshman (meaning I was a sophomore academically but in my first year athletically), all that changed. I wasn't sure if it was because people expected us to win or because I was such good gossip, but suddenly twice as many people started showing up for games. These fans weren't just parents or bored students, either; they were the young girls who'd lined up after my volleyball matches and asked me to sign autographs. They were people for whom basketball actually *meant* something. They didn't come only to experience a thrilling victory—because sometimes we weren't even expected to win—but because they really enjoyed the dynamics of the sport.

Believe me, I did too. From the moment I started practicing, I loved being back.

One of the things that's most often said about me is that on the court my face doesn't reveal anything. I might be in agony over the basket I just missed—or I might be head-over-heels happy about blocking a shot—but my face will be a blank slate. During my freshman season I looked as serious as always during every game. But the truth was that inside I was beaming.

The team dynamics just *felt* different. On the court we were dedicated players, but off it we were regular old college students. No one treated us like we were slacking off if we didn't think about basketball 24/7, and I wasn't hard on myself if I decided to do something like go shopping before a game instead of resting to "conserve my energy." (Sheesh. I was *such* a serious kid!)

During my first season, we attended an away game over the Thanksgiving break. After we all ate Thanksgiving dinner together, our coaches decided to put the freshman players on the spot.

"All of you have to come up with a skit," one of the assistant coaches announced. "And it better be funny! You have half an hour to figure this out starting . . . now!"

I'm not the world's best actress—or even close to it—but I love watching movies. One of my favorites is *The Break-Up* with Jennifer Aniston and Vince Vaughn. I know pretty much every scene line-for-line, so when the other freshman players and I huddled together to figure out what to perform, I knew the answer right away.

"Let's do our best impression of the scene where Jennifer Aniston's gay brother teaches everyone a cappella at the dinner table."

We might have had only a half hour to practice, but we nailed it. People were practically on the floor laughing. I was so proud of myself. But more than that, I realized how much I was growing as a person. For the first time in forever, I was feeling relaxed around my teammates.

I was doing well on the court too. Taking a year off hadn't broken my stride, and I averaged 26.7 points a game, which was the third-highest Division 1 average in the country. In a game against James Madison University in February, I scored a record-high fifty-four points, which was the highest single-game score of any female Division 1 player all season. At the end of the year, I was named the CAA's Rookie of the Year, and I was the first player ever in UD history to be named an Associated Press All-American, landing a spot on the third team.

Our team wasn't the Elena Delle Donne Show either. If it

had been, I'm sure I would have been unhappy because I just couldn't stand all that pressure. Instead we played beautifully *together*. And while we didn't get a bid to the NCAA tournament, the season was a huge improvement over the previous one, and we finished with a 25–12 record. We left that year on a high, feeling deep in our bones that the 2010–2011 season was going to be the best we'd ever had.

Thankfully, I had no idea that I might not be in my prime. I was given no warning that the winter of 2010 was going to be the most physically and emotionally challenging period in my entire life.

Chapter Twelve

Lyme Disease, Take Two

In 2010 my sophomore season started out beautifully. In the preseason I was named to three watch lists, and by early December the UD women's team had won six out of our first seven games, most by double digits. We were filling up the Bob almost to capacity, and we were completely in sync during practices and games. In fact, Coach Martin was saying that we were the best team she'd seen in her more than 250 games as head coach.

The only problem was that a week or so after Thanksgiving, I started feeling terrible. And on December 19, at an away game against Penn State, I fell completely apart.

Ever since I was a kid, I'd always done as much as possible to take care of my body to prevent illnesses. I ate right, and I saw my doctor regularly. If a pain in my shoulder or my hamstring—or anywhere, really—was bothering me, I'd go see a doctor immediately. And to prevent injuries or illnesses, I'd always stretch well, warm up, drink lots of water, take my vitamins, and get my flu shot. After all, basketball season is right smack in the middle of flu season, and the last thing

I wanted was to miss a game because of something I likely could have prevented.

A day or two before our game against Penn State, my body started to ache all over. I wasn't just uncomfortable either; I was having deep muscle pains, especially in my arms and legs. I talked to Coach Martin about it, and she booked me an appointment with the team doctor right away. He took my temperature and checked my vitals, and he couldn't find anything wrong with me.

"You don't have a fever or any visible signs of an infection like the flu," he said, "so I think you've just been practicing and playing too hard. Keep an eye on how you're feeling and get some rest. If you need to sit out some practices or games, do it."

After totally burning out twice in my life, I knew my body well enough to realize when it was time to take a break. My aches and pains weren't constant, so I wasn't convinced I had to sideline myself just yet. In fact, when Coach Martin asked me if I felt well enough to start against Penn State, I didn't hesitate to say yes.

Unfortunately, I felt awful from the moment the whistle blew. After I tipped the ball, I just couldn't move as fast as I usually did. It was like I was walking through mud. When I passed the ball to a teammate, every joint and muscle in my body started to scream. After the ball came back to me, I began to dribble more slowly and deliberately, like I was doing it in slow motion, and when it came time to make a shot, I could barely lift my arms more than halfway. The basketball felt like it weighed ten thousand pounds, and I practically had to throw my whole body forward when I lunged for the basket. *Ugh.*

Of course I missed the shot. The ball didn't even come close to the net. Eleven minutes into the game, I turned and limped toward the sideline.

"Coach," I whispered, "I don't know what's wrong with me, but I need to sit out the rest of the game. I think I'm going to pass out."

In the sixteen years I'd been playing basketball, I'd never—not once—left a game midstream. But there was nothing else I could do. My body felt foreign, like it had been invaded by something that wanted to knock it down and then stomp all over it. From the bench I watched the game unfold, but it seemed like it was a million miles away. When we lost, I didn't even feel sad; I was too busy imagining that my head had been wrapped in plastic, because I thought I was going to suffocate.

That night I went back to campus, crawled into bed, and slept for twelve hours. When I woke the next morning, I could hardly turn over because my pain was so unbearable, and my head was throbbing like someone was beating it with a bat. After about twenty minutes of trying, I finally rolled over, extended my arm, and pressed a few buttons on my phone. I heard a ringing, then my mother's voice.

"Mom?" I groaned.

"Elena?" she said. "Are you feeling okay? I was so worried about you after the game. Did you get some sleep?"

"Come get me," I said. "Please, come quick. I need you to take me to the hospital. I think I'm dying."

Mom arrived within a half hour, unshowered and wearing no makeup. After she practically carried me through the door and loaded me into the car, she drove me straight to my primary care physician. A nurse ushered me in, took me to a small, private room, and checked me out. Less than ten minutes later, I met with my doctor.

"We're going to run some tests," he said, "But I don't think you're in any immediate danger. Your blood pressure is fine, and so is your temperature. We're just going to monitor your heart to be sure."

The doctor and nurse hooked me up to a heart monitor and gave me a pain reliever so that I'd feel more comfortable. I drifted off into an uneasy sleep, and when I woke up, a nurse was asking if she could draw some blood. I nodded my head— still in terrible pain—but I couldn't speak. *Just please find out what's wrong with me,* I thought, *because I can't go on like this.*

Since my condition didn't get worse, I went home with my mom rather than to the hospital. I decided to stay there. I couldn't take care of myself, so I needed my mom and dad— and Gene, who'd just moved back to Wilmington to work with my dad—to do it for me. The next day I hardly ate anything, and for what felt like a week, I slept eighteen hours a day. I couldn't hold a conversation or make decisions, since my brain was so foggy, and almost every day I'd position myself in a quiet, dark room and stay there all day, paralyzed from a migraine.

Yet the test results from the doctor came back and revealed nothing.

"It's not a bacterial infection, and we can't find any evidence of a virus or parasite," the doctor said. "So we're not really sure what it is. I recommend seeing some specialists, like an infectious disease doctor, a cardiologist, and even a back specialist, since you're having so much discomfort in your back."

After years and years of dealing with all the mysteries and challenges surrounding Lizzie's health, my parents absolutely refused to give up. They knew that I wouldn't have felt sick or hurt for no reason, so they were determined to find out what was wrong with me. Over the next few weeks, they scheduled appointments with all of the doctors that my primary care physician recommended. I saw all of them and donated what felt like a gallon of blood. I got an MRI on my brain and even had a stress test, which I fainted in the middle of. Yet test after test after test showed nothing. I'd made it my full-time job to get a diagnosis, and drove hundreds of miles to do it, yet I still didn't get an answer. After almost a month my family and I weren't just scared or frustrated; we were furious—especially when doctors started writing me off.

"Elena's clearly been through a lot," one doctor said. "I think she's just depressed. This is probably all in her head."

"Nothing's wrong with her," said another.

And finally: "It must be chronic fatigue syndrome, which means your playing days are over."

Now, I've had huge ups and downs in my life, and when

I left UConn, I could hardly string two thoughts together, so I know what depression feels like. This was not it. There was something terribly wrong with me physically, and if we couldn't find out what it was, I was positive I was going to die.

Worse, some doctors thought so too.

"It might be a neurological condition like multiple sclerosis," a neurologist told me. "So we need to run more tests. MS only gets worse—not better—so you need to know as soon as possible so you can prepare yourself."

Luckily, those tests came back negative. But I still didn't have any answers.

While lying in bed aching all over, suffering through migraines, and sleeping like it was my life's mission, I'd missed ten basketball games. Some days, when I was feeling halfway good, I'd have my mom drive me to the Bob, and I'd try to train with my team. But it was never easy. I was just too sore and tired.

After about six weeks of shuttling from one doctor to another, with no diagnosis or even a sense of what we should explore next, my mom announced that she thought we should see a Lyme disease specialist.

"A friend of mine read in the paper about you being sick," she said, "and she suggested it might be a flare-up of Lyme disease."

"There's no way," I shot back. "I got over that two years ago. It's not a chronic condition, so it can't come back."

Like I said before, Mom refused to take no for an answer when it came to her kids' health, and she knew that sometimes what seems to be impossible can happen. For example, some doctors had been sure Lizzie would never be able to lift her head on her own or ever be able to walk. Of course she does both.

Mom had gone ahead and scheduled an appointment with a nurse practitioner in Lancaster County, Pennsylvania. Her name was Rita Rhoads, and she owned a clinic that specialized in tick-borne illnesses. It would take me a good hour to drive there, but, like Mom, I didn't care. I was desperate. I would have flown halfway around the country if it would help me get to the bottom of what was wrong with me.

My dad is super-knowledgeable when it comes to health, and he always asks the right questions, so he decided to go with me. He'd also spent the entire month researching tick-borne illnesses and had a ton of questions for Rita.

From the moment we pulled up to the Integrative Health Consults offices, though, I was just as skeptical as I'd been when Mom had first said the words "Lyme disease flare-up." First off, Christiana, Pennsylvania, had maybe a thousand people in it. It was in the middle of Amish country, and we'd passed more horse-drawn wagons than cars on the way there. Second, it was the furthest thing from a hospital—or even a doctor's office—I'd ever seen. Rita Rhoads saw patients in a small blue vinyl-sided house on the side of a busy country road. *Is this for real?* I thought. But I figured my parents knew best, so I decided to just go with it.

I'd filled out a long questionnaire about my health before I'd gotten on the road to drive to Pennsylvania, and when Rita Rhoads walked in and sat across from me in an overstuffed chair, she was clearly prepared. But was I? Rita looked more like a country nurse than an expert in tick-borne diseases. I wasn't just worried about what I was going to say; I also wasn't sure I could trust her. But when she started asking me questions, I realized how wrong I was.

"I've reviewed your paperwork," she said, "and you show all the symptoms of Lyme disease. I know you had it before, and it's very possible that this could be a recurrence or be connected with other tick-borne illnesses like bartonella, babesia, mycoplasma, or anaplasma."

I looked at her, wide-eyed. "But I thought that was impossible. Doctors told me that once Lyme disease is cured, it doesn't come back."

"I don't agree with that. There are a lot of studies about Lyme disease infection in animals, and we know that sometimes the bacteria hides, then reappears when the body is under stress. The first line of treatment for Lyme disease is antibiotics, and doctors don't want to keep people on them for a long time. So they try to find another diagnosis."

"Why is that?" I asked. "What's wrong with being on antibiotics for a long time?"

"Sometimes the side effects from antibiotics are worse than the disease. That's why I treat chronic Lyme disease sufferers with supplements and direct them toward a healthy diet and lifestyle. You need to boost up your immune system to fight an infection, and healthy living—rather than antibiotics—can do that. But first things first. Let's talk about you."

I sat in stunned silence for just a minute, till my dad nudged me in the side. During every single one of my many doctors appointments over the last six weeks, no doctor had sat with me for more than five minutes. They'd taken my blood and looked at my chart, then told me I was making my illness up, was depressed, or might be suffering from a life-threatening neurological or autoimmune condition. Yet here I was, in the middle of nowhere Pennsylvania, with a woman who wanted to ask about *me*. She wanted to know about more than my white blood cell count, and she didn't care about probabilities or what was considered impossible by modern science. She just wanted me to be well, and even though she hardly knew me, she trusted me.

I'm pretty soft-spoken most of the time, and sometimes I hesitate to really get talking unless I'm asked questions. But with Rita, I let it all hang out. I told her about the summer after my senior year of high school, when I first got Lyme disease, and all the stress I'd been under recently, having returned to basketball. I talked about my workouts and my diet. I told her I thought I was dying, and I went into a ton of detail about the game against Penn State, when I couldn't even lift up my arms to shoot a basket. When I was finally finished, I think I'd talked for ten straight minutes, but for the first time since I'd gotten sick, I actually felt hope.

"This is so interesting," Rita said. "I'm going to ask to take some blood, but I should have results soon. If this is what I think it is, we're going to come up with a course of treatment that's specific to you. When that happens, you'll be following it for the rest of your life."

You might think that hearing that I had a chronic condition was scary, but trust me, it wasn't. All I wanted was answers, and I was willing to spend the rest of my life doing absolutely anything and everything I could so that I didn't get sick again.

The drive back to Wilmington was one of the happiest hours of my life. I think that having a medical professional tell me that she might know the answer to my problems woke something up in me, and suddenly I started to feel alive again. By the time we got home, I was thinking more clearly than I had in weeks. I sat down with my dad that night, ready to talk.

"Dad," I said, "I think some higher power is testing me right now. I'm pretty sure it wants me to figure out if I'm really, really committed to basketball. If I make it through being sick, maybe it'll give me another chance to play."

Dad laughed. "Well, that's one way to think of it."

"Dad!" I smiled. "I'm sort of serious. Being this sick has made me realize how much I miss playing. When I'm on the court, I feel great."

I went to bed that night determined to get back to practice soon. *I have to,* I thought as I closed my eyes. *I know what I'm capable of.*

But before I did anything, I needed a diagnosis and a course of treatment. *Please let Rita call me soon,* I thought just before I drifted off to sleep. *I want to know what this is.*

Two days later Rita called.

"Your blood tests show trace amounts of bacteria related to Lyme disease and the other tick-borne infections I mentioned in my office, so I'm going to put you on antibiotics now. I'll call in a prescription, but I'll need you to come back here next week so we can discuss a course of supplements."

I pretty much screamed. "Thank you! Thank you!" Then I set up another appointment, hung up the phone, and started to cry.

I'm not crazy, I thought. *All those doctors were wrong.*

I took antibiotics for three weeks, but I felt better almost immediately. I was so improved, in fact, that I moved back onto campus, started practicing with my team again, and on February 3 played a full twenty-six minutes in a home game against Northeastern. We won.

I'm back! I thought. I celebrated as my teammates crowded around me. Winning a game had never felt so good.

At my next appointment with Rita, she put me on a strict regimen of supplements. Every single day, to keep the infections at bay, I'd take fifty pills and supplements—like vitamin C, Viragraphis, biotin, ATP Fuel, and probiotics.

"We'll tweak this over time," she said. "But right now I want to focus on strengthening your immune system."

She also recommended that I cut out gluten, red meat, caffeine, dairy, and sugar. These foods are known to cause inflammation, and since I'd been suffering joint pain, the last thing I needed was for my joints to swell up after eating a meat pizza washed down with three Cokes.

"You also need to keep your stress under control," she said. "Too much pressure weakens your immune system and might lead to a flare-up."

"That's yet another reason to avoid burning out," I answered. "It's not just mental. Being too hard on myself is going to affect my health, too."

"Absolutely," Rita said. "Be good to yourself. You deserve it."

I knew I did. I realized it was my right to be healthy and happy. I was young, and I wanted to be at 100 percent. After all, basketball had once again become my passion, and I wasn't just ready to finish my college season. I was also poised to hit the international stage.

Chapter Thirteen

Elena International

I can't say that the rest of my second season was easy. In fact, coming back to the basketball court after almost two months away was even harder than the eleven months I'd taken off during my first year playing. While I'd been sick, my muscles had gotten weak, and I'd lost much of the confidence I'd felt on the court for the past season and a half. Every time I yawned, felt a pain in my joints, or noticed that my head was fuzzy, I worried, *Am I sick again?*

Even my coach and teammates were concerned. The team had struggled while I was away, losing seven of the twelve games I'd missed, and our hopes of being CAA champions and making it to the NCAA championship were growing dim. Would me being back help turn that losing streak around? Or was that too much pressure to put on a player who was probably running at half capacity, and who might get sick if she pushed herself too hard?

It's my choice to make, I decided. *It doesn't matter what anyone else thinks or is concerned about. Worrying about what's expected of me will only make me burn out, so I'm just going to trust myself and play my best.*

I must have put some good vibes out in the world, because, luckily, our team and our style of play began clicking. After our victory against Northeastern, we won our next three games, the last against William and Mary in a nail-biter that ended in overtime. We lost a few games after that, but when we went into the CAA tournament, we were confident. We were playing cohesively, and all of us were feeling great, especially me.

We almost won the CAA tournament, but we fell to James Madison in the finals. Still, we had a good enough record to advance to the National Invitation Tournament (NIT). We lost in the first round, but we still walked off the court with our heads high.

We did the best we could in a really tough season, I thought. *And I know we'll do better next year.*

I wasn't fooling myself, though. I knew that if I was going to help UD be the best in the CAA and go to the NCAA tournament, I was going to have to be in tip-top shape. Not just physically, either; I realized I needed to mentally challenge myself to a higher level of play than I could find in regular college hoops. I needed to expose myself to different players, new coaches, and competitors who played differently than anyone I'd encountered before.

Luckily, I was going to have my chance, and it would happen sooner than I'd ever imagined it would.

The World University Games are an every-other-year college-aged tournament run under USA Basketball. You might not have heard of them, but they're a huge deal. In fact, they're second only to the Olympics in terms of worldwide participants, and in 2011, I had the chance to be among them.

I was one of fourteen college players who'd been invited to a training camp at the US Olympic Training Center in Colorado Springs. After three days of practices, we'd find out which twelve of us would advance to the World University Games, which were being held in Shenzhen, China, in the middle of August. Not only would this be my first shot at an international tournament, but it would be the most high-profile position I'd ever had on a team.

That was, *if* I made the team.

As you know, I was still recovering, physically and emotionally. I was open about it too, telling my parents how frustrated I was that I wasn't at 100 percent, especially when I had the biggest audition of my life ahead of me.

"Just work as hard as you can," they said, "but don't kill yourself. We don't want you to burn out or get sick again."

That's what I have to remember, I kept telling myself as I drilled into my head the fact that Lyme disease flare-ups could be brought on by stress. *Burning out isn't just emotional for me anymore. It's physical. If I push myself too hard for too long, I'm going to get really, really sick again.*

I refocused my energy and never forced myself to the point of exhaustion. I took my supplements, got my joints limber with really dynamic warm-ups, and was strict with my new diet. I began to listen to my body in a way I hadn't before, and over the course of the spring and early summer, I started to see real results. My assistant coach, Tiara Malcom, did too, and she approached me one day to tell me.

"You've developed more in the last few months than any player I've ever seen. You're at the top of your game, Elena. Seriously, watch out, world."

I just hoped the coaches at the Colorado Springs training camp agreed.

As you can probably guess, American women have typically dominated basketball internationally. The sport was invented in the US, we have the largest professional women's league, and basketball is a part of our culture more than almost any other nation on earth. But by 2011 that had started to change. In Eastern Europe and Asia, basketball had become a huge sport, and even Australia produced massive stars like Lauren Jackson. In the World University Games, the USA had won eight gold medals since their first tournament visit in 1973, but they were by no means a shoo-in to win every year. The whole team knew we'd be facing some tough competition. To increase the pressure, we were defending the gold medal that the USA team had won in 2009, and winning twice in a row was something the USA had never done.

The head coach for the US team was Bill Fennelly, who was from Iowa State University. It was his job to watch fourteen women practice for three straight days, then announce the two players who hadn't made the team and send them home. I knew that his eliminating only two people meant that my chances for making it to the games was good, but when I looked out onto the court and saw my competition, it was scary.

These are the best players in college hoops, I thought.

Yet after three of the hardest, most rewarding days of my life, Coach Fennelly announced that I'd made the team. Eleven of the top college players in the country and I would remain in Colorado Springs for another week of practice. Then we'd fly to China, get adjusted to the time change, and play our first game on August 13.

Just six months after an illness that had almost sidelined me forever, I hadn't just made my basketball comeback. I was about to play with the world's best female college basketball players in a country halfway around the globe.

Chapter Fourteen

China

Now that I play in the WNBA and have competed in the Olympics, I've found myself in games with all kinds of players, a lot of whom are far more skilled than I am. But as members of an elite league, we're all on a level playing field. In 2011, though, a big part of me felt like the comeback kid from the small university in one of the smallest states in the country. Did that mean that I was out to prove something? Not really. I was just humbled to be on a team with amazing women from powerhouse schools, like Nneka Ogwumike from Stanford and Skylar Diggins from Notre Dame.

The wonderful thing about basketball—or any team sport—is that when you're on a team together, you're playing as one. No one is—or should be—trying to show up anyone else. You just want to play up each other's strengths, make up for any weaknesses that come out on the court, and sink as many baskets as you can. Ego shouldn't matter. Performing your best should.

In the World University Games in August 2011, that's what happened. The USA team totally steamrolled the competition in the first four games, defeating Brazil, then Slovakia, then Great Britain, and finally Finland by more than fifty points each game.

I was feeling great on the court. In the game against Brazil, I'd been the leading scorer with seventeen points, and over all of the initial games, I was the top rebounder. I think listening to my body had helped, but more than that, I was working with a team whose basketball skills were so impressive that, for the first time in a long time, I wasn't expected to be the best player on the court. My team wouldn't lack anything (or almost anything!) if I sat out for a few minutes—or even an entire game. Every single player on the USA team brought a very particular kind of leadership to the court, and each and every one of us learned something that elevated our play to a higher level.

We were set to compete against Australia in the semi-final round, and if we beat them, we'd advance to the gold medal game. We knew they were a good team; they were big and physical, and they'd medaled twice before in the World University Games. But even though we were prepared, they put up an incredible fight.

USA hadn't trailed a team the entire tournament, but the moment the ball was tipped, Australia took off. They grabbed the lead right away and held it till there were just over seven minutes left in the first quarter. Honestly, we were shocked at how aggressively they were playing. *They must think we underestimated them,* I remember saying to myself. *And maybe we did?* Right then, though, all of us decided to step it up a notch, and Nneka Ogwumike nailed two foul shots, tying the game. Then I made a jumper, followed by a three-pointer, giving us a five-point lead.

We went on a 10–2 tear after that, but Australia answered with a 9–4 run, and by the end of the first quarter, we were up by only three points. The second quarter wasn't much better either. While we were always in the lead, Australia kept the pressure on, and neither team ever scored more than four points in a stretch. By halftime we were up by only four.

We have to play stronger, I thought as we headed into the locker room. *We can beat them. We have to.*

Coach Finnelly had said throughout the tournament that we tended to play our worst during the third quarter, and as he started talking to us, he stressed that.

"This quarter, don't make the same mistakes you have in the last few games. Come out strong and stay that way. You're all faster than them, so make some baskets quickly, then wear them down."

When the whistle blew for the third quarter, we did just that. Skylar Diggins and I scored inside the paint right away, and Devereaux Peters followed with a jumper. Then we capped a 9–0 run when Shekinna Stricklen sunk a three-pointer.

We're pulling away, I thought. *This is how it's done.*

From that moment on Australia was playing catch-up. We did just as Coach Finnelly had ordered and outran and out-rebounded them, but with almost five minutes left in the quarter, Australia went on another run. With 3:50 left in the third quarter, we'd only extended our lead to five points.

We knew we had to change the course of the game in the final stretch, so when the fourth quarter began, we started pushing harder than we had all game. Within a few minutes we scored nine unanswered points, and we didn't let up after that. We finally locked into how to cut across the paint and set screens, and we outmuscled Australia using that knowledge. When the final buzzer went off, we'd won, 79–67, and we couldn't have been more relieved.

"Even though it was sometimes close, you played hard, like a team in the semis should," Coach Finnelly said afterward. "You had to *earn* this game, and you did that." Then he paused. "But we're going to have to change our strategy in the gold medal matchup. Taiwan is scrappy and fast."

We had only two days to practice before the game, but it turned out that was plenty. The gold medal game against Taiwan was absolutely no contest. We outmaneuvered and outmuscled them, and we won the game easily, 101–66.

What amazed me more than the fact that I'd actually won internationally, though, was just how much playing at a high level—with the best players in the country—hadn't led me to burn out. You'd think that with all that pressure, I would have, but I didn't. *I think that's because I wasn't always expected to be the best,* I realized. Sure, I'd ended up being the leading scorer overall, but in the final game against Taiwan, Nneka Ogwumike had sunk more baskets than me. I hadn't *always* been the top performer, and the game hadn't all been on my shoulders. Instead I'd relaxed into team play, where one person's near foul-out or series of missed baskets can be made up for by someone else's three-point shot.

Learning to depend on other people—all the time—is what I need to do, I thought. *That's how UD is going to have a great season.*

Chapter Fifteen

Vocal Leadership

I took that philosophy back with me to campus for my junior season, and suddenly basketball filled up all my thoughts. For years it had been my life's work, but in my third year playing basketball as a Blue Hen, it became my *life*. And anyone who knows me knows how much I love being alive.

Viewing basketball as a team effort rather than a sport that I had to carry on my shoulders alone also made me think about my role on the court. Sure, I knew I could shoot free throws and almost never miss, that my height meant I could block more shots than not, and I was super-skilled at making three-pointers, but what else could I add to my team that I hadn't already? How else could I help elevate our level of play so that we could be CAA champions and advance to the NCAA tournament? I wanted our success to be as a team, not just *about* me or *because* of me.

Before summer training even started, I sat down to talk to John Noonan about these questions. For more than a decade John had been my mentor and my basketball guide, and I knew he'd come up with some great advice.

"I'm playing better than ever," I said, "but I need to do something else. Something more."

John didn't even hesitate to answer. Clearly he'd been thinking about my role on the Blue Hens as much as I had.

"Elena, you are a natural team leader. Everyone knows that. But I've watched you practice and play, and you don't express that. I think you need to assert yourself everywhere: in the locker room, in the huddle, and on the court. You need to talk more, to get people pumped up. You know the game and how to play it, so say it out loud. This year I think it's time for you to become a vocal leader."

For just a moment I sat and thought about what John had said. I've always been quieter than most people, and I hate being critical or telling people what to do. Maybe it's because I'm a third child, so when I was born, I learned to fit into my family rather than take charge of it. I trusted Gene to be the loud one, and for everyone to step up to whatever Lizzie needed. But right then I realized John was right. If I wanted UD to advance and play at a higher level—a level I'd proven that summer that I could reach on a team—I had to speak up.

"You're right," I said. "I hate being the bad cop, but I know how my teammates can play better, so I have to tell them that." Then I looked him straight in the face and made my goal for the coming season. "I'm going to be a vocal leader this year."

Right from our first game, it was clear that I could be. I started getting my teammates pumped up before games, and when the whistle blew, it was I who would yell to a teammate who seemed hesitant to pass the ball or attempt an unlikely shot. I started encouraging my team to take risks, to reach higher, and to play more aggressively. I decided I didn't want to be just a physical presence on the court. I wanted people to hear me too. After all, if I relied on my fragile body alone, it might fail me like it had the year before.

I sensed a change in my team's energy right away. We got on the court, we challenged one another, and we started winning. In November we beat the University of Rhode Island, then Penn State, then Villanova, then more teams after that. Thanksgiving passed, and by the time Christmas came around, we'd won ten in a row and still hadn't lost. The Bob had moveable bleachers that were used only for huge events like graduation, and maintenance rolled them out as average fan attendance soared from about two thousand to almost four thousand. A local middle school class used women's basketball tickets as a prize for whichever student finished their required reading first, and we heard reports that students had never read faster in their lives. I found out that students and faculty were buying season tickets in droves. Sure, my parents did that, but it was pretty much unheard of for everyone else.

Suddenly the Blue Hens were the hottest ticket in town. Even though that came with pressure, I didn't let it get to me. I was too happy that my team was winning.

Unfortunately, we finally fell to the University of Maryland in a late December nail-biter. The game was so action-packed, with each side playing so aggressively, that the media said it actually had the feel of an NCAA tournament game. Maryland was ranked number five in the nation and was on an unbeaten streak just like us, and we knew from the beginning that it would be an uphill battle. Still, we played with all our hearts, and I couldn't have been prouder of the team.

In the New Year, as we started conference play, we got right back to winning, and the crowds kept coming. US Vice President Joe Biden, who is a University of Delaware alum and lived in Wilmington when he wasn't in Washington, watched us beat Drexel in late January. We showed up in the campus weekly e-mail about upcoming school events—something that had never happened before—and even people who had never seen a basketball game in their lives came to watch us. I was on cloud nine during each and every game, but did I hate the spotlight? Was the pressure bearing down on me? Not for a second. I'd made a deliberate choice about this school, this team, and this season, and I felt confident in all of it.

I was nearing a career milestone too. At the beginning of a February game against Hofstra, I was pretty sure I was going to score my two-thousandth collegiate point. I was the leading scorer in the NCAA, averaging about twenty-eight points a game, so unless I had to sideline myself for one reason or another, I thought I'd do it.

It's going to happen sooner or later, I told myself, *so don't let it get to you.*

It didn't. Even though there was a line of shirtless male Hofstra students standing in the first row behind the goal, taunting me while they held up printouts of Geno Auriemma's head, I sank ball after ball, scoring forty-two points in the game and breaking the two-thousand mark. It wasn't like the time I broke the high school foul shot record, when I almost melted from the weight I felt. This time, breaking two thousand was all a part of helping my team win. It wasn't just *my* success or *my* milestone. It was all a part of leading UD toward a victory.

UD finished the season undefeated in the CAA. And when we played in the CAA tournament, we won all three games by double digits. We were going to advance to the NCAA tournament for the first time since 2008, and we'd done it as a team.

Chapter Sixteen

NCAA Tournament Debut

Our opponent in the first round of the NCAA tournament was the University of Arkansas at Little Rock, and we were expected to win. They were a fourteenth-ranked seed from a tiny conference, while we were third in our region. We were known as an up-and-coming powerhouse with only one loss under our belt, and we were fresh off a tournament we'd dominated.

But strange things happen in the early round of tournaments, so we vowed to play like we meant it. And we did; we won 73–42.

Our second-round opponent was the University of Kansas, and to say we were nervous would be an understatement. First off, Delaware had never before advanced beyond the first round of the NCAA tournament, so we were in totally uncharted territory. Even though Kansas was a number-eleven seed, making them the underdog, they'd been to the tournament before. They were a much bigger school than us, with a men's basketball program that was always one of the best. We were still, in everybody's mind, the little guys. Second, we knew we were making headlines. We had an almost unbeaten record and the nation's leading scorer (me). Because people were *still* talking about me leaving UConn, we were a juicy story. Even the president was talking us up! In an interview with ESPN, Barack Obama mentioned that in his bracket he'd picked UD to advance all the way to the Elite Eight. Was he just trying to make Vice President Biden happy? We'll never know, but, oh boy, did it keep us on our toes!

There's a big difference between the kind of pressure I felt when I got to UConn and the kind I felt before the game against Kansas, though. At UConn part of the reason why I burned out is because I felt all alone. When I looked around me, all I saw were women who wanted to play basketball for the rest of their lives. I imagined that none of them thought it was okay to fail. At UConn we were all expected to be the best, and losing just wasn't an option.

As I sat in the locker room before one of the biggest games of my life, I realized that most of my UD teammates knew they'd leave basketball after college, so a part of them was playing just because it was fun. They understood that it was entirely possible we might lose—and that was okay. We'd made it further than we ever had before, and we'd try our absolute hardest to make it through to another round.

We were prepared. Coach Martin had made sure of it.

"Kansas is going to be all over us," she said just before the game. "Especially you, Elena. You're going to be double- and triple-teamed, so be ready."

That was nothing new, so I didn't think much of it. What

did concern me, though, was the attitude the Jayhawks probably had. They'd lost their leading scorer earlier in the season
and had suffered a string of defeats because of it, so making it this far in the tournament was a huge deal for them. I
wondered: *Are they going to be extra confident because they've
already been through so much adversity and succeeded?* I had
no idea, so I figured I had to be prepared for anything.

From the second the whistle blew, Coach Martin's words
held true. I had defenders on top of me everywhere I turned.
They came at me all at once—one, two, and three at a time—
waving their arms, pushing toward me, and trying to make
me as uncomfortable as possible. One of my strategies has
always been to put on my game face—serious, so no one can
see how I'm feeling—and I doubled up on that. But when I
wasn't being swarmed by Kansas defenders, I was acting
like the vocal leader I told myself I should be, yelling and
encouraging my team.

For the first half of the game, it worked. We entered the
locker room leading Kansas 37–31.

"You're playing great," Coach Martin said to us, "but I can
tell that Kansas has a fire inside them. So don't stop hustling."

Sure enough, in the second half things started to unravel.
I was shooting well—50 percent from the field—and my
rebounding was just as good as always, but we couldn't pull
our defense together. We looked tired, running to catch up
with an ever-faster Kansas, and we weren't clicking as a team.
Defense had been a huge strength for us all season, and when
it started to fail us, we looked lost. A Kansas player named

Natalie Knight made shot after shot after shot, and we couldn't hold her back. *We've got to try something new. We have to get morale back up,* I thought, and I screamed at my teammates to do just that.

Kansas went on a 19–6 run, and soon they were up 53–43.

If our defense keeps falling apart, I have to step into high gear.

In high school, being the success or failure of a team was one of my least favorite feelings in the world. The last thing I ever wanted was the pressure that comes not just with being the best, but with being the *only* option. I honestly don't know, at that point in the game, if I actually *was* our team's only hope, but I didn't care. I'd matured and moved beyond worrying about everything being up to me. I just wanted us to win, so I was going to do everything I possibly could to make that happen.

I scored twelve points right in a row, and the score was 59–57. We were only two points from tying the game.

Kansas answered right away, though, and soon they were up 68–57. Our defense was just no match for them, and we couldn't keep up with how well they were shooting for the net. By the time I heard the final buzzer, the score was 70–64, and we'd lost the game.

As I walked toward the sidelines, I could feel hot tears coming into my eyes. The most remarkable season I'd ever experienced was over, but I was disappointed for reasons I'd never expected.

I don't care what mistakes I made, I thought. *I'm over being critical of myself. I'm just sad that the seniors on this team have to say good-bye now. We had so much fun this year, and now it's over.*

Chapter Seventeen

Seize Every Moment

Because I hadn't played basketball my freshman year, my first season with the Blue Hens had been as a redshirt freshman. That meant that during my sophomore year, I was in my first year of basketball eligibility, but I was in my second year academically. By the time I played against Kansas in the NCAA tournament, I was the same age as the seniors on the squad. I'd been at Delaware for four years, and I could graduate if I wanted to. There was more at stake, though; if I decided to leave UD, I could enter the WNBA draft.

My life after college wasn't a decision I took lightly. When I'd chosen to give up basketball forever three years before, I'd told myself to come up with a backup plan, and that was special education. At Delaware I'd studied hard in my special ed classes and had held internships, and when I hung out with Lizzie and her friends, I'd used the skills I'd been learning. I knew—even when I was at the top of my college game—that I had the option to leave basketball again and still have a fulfilling career as a teacher or therapist. Basketball didn't have to be everything.

I *wanted* it to be, though. Part of me was surprised, but I'd grown to love it. I'd decided to make it my career—not because it was all I knew how to do, but because it was all my heart longed for.

But was it something I'd dive into a year early, before I'd given the Blue Hens a full four seasons? Even though the WNBA recruiting class that year wasn't as competitive as it would be the following year, and I probably would have been a top draft pick, I refused to consider it. I was having way too much fun playing basketball.

After my burnout I'd realized that having a good time was the key to avoiding another collapse. Enjoying something—then just going with it—was what would make me happy, and happiness was the antidote to too much pressure. If I got stressed, I might start to hate basketball, or, worse, I might have another relapse of Lyme disease.

I was onto a good thing at UD, happier than I'd ever been before in my life. That's why I knew deep in my soul that it wasn't time to leave. I was going to stay another year and work as hard as possible to see the Blue Hens reach the Sweet Sixteen in the NCAA tournament. I knew it was possible. We had a terrific incoming class, and the sophomores, juniors, and seniors were still riding the high of our previous season. They wanted to do better than last year as much as I did.

The season started out in November beautifully. In non-conference play, we defeated the University of Rhode Island and then Penn State, both at home. We had five days off until our next game, and we were going to work out and practice steadily till then. But, unfortunately, I could tell something wasn't right. It wasn't with the team either; it was with me.

Ever since the agony I'd gone through getting diagnosed with chronic Lyme disease, I'd been vigilant about making sure I was on top of my health. I was strict about my diet, took all my supplements, and if something in my body was bothering me, I wouldn't brush it off. I couldn't. I'd take a day off to visit Rita Rhoads if I had to, or I'd rest in bed all day, monitoring my symptoms. When I woke up on the morning of November 20, my head was throbbing and my joints were screaming. I could barely roll to one side to get out of bed, and when I finally did, I stumbled toward the phone.

"Coach Martin," I whispered, "I'm having a flare-up. I can't play Providence tonight, so I need to take some time to rest."

I've been blessed with a lot of understanding people since I got sick, but I think Coach Martin never really understood my Lyme disease. When I'd first gotten my diagnosis two years before, she downplayed it, and even warned me that I'd be remembered as a high school has-been if I didn't get my act together.

This time she was silent on the phone, and then she told me to get to the gym for practice.

I hung up the phone and punched my fist into the wall. I was just so tired of feeling that she wasn't listening. I also realized that I'd be justifying my illness to skeptical people for who knows how long, and that left a hollow feeling in my gut. Finally, I hated not having a clue as to how long this flare-up would last. All I knew was that I had to take a short break from basketball, rest up, and get better.

This time I may be sick for a week or a month—or even three months. I may miss the rest of the season! I have no idea today, and I won't for the rest of my life either.

Right at that moment I think I accepted how unknown the future was for me. Sure, if my health was perfect and I never injured myself so badly that I couldn't play again, I'd probably have a career in basketball for the next decade. But with Lyme disease breathing down my neck, the prospect of leaving the sport again was very real. Every time I felt my muscles scream for no reason, my joints crack, my head throb, or my vision weaken, it might be a flare-up, and it might stop me in my tracks—forever. I had a chronic condition, and that meant it would be with me, always keeping me on my toes, for the rest of my life.

Realizing you're sick—even when you're feeling great—can be a depressing thought for a lot of people. I think elite athletes, especially, like to feel superhuman, but we have to understand that we can break as easily as everybody else. I refuse to let that get me down. I have a sister who's been severely compromised since the moment she came into the world, and she still feels joy all the time. Lizzie lives in the moment, delighting in the beautiful things she can smell and feel, and the family and friends that care for her. During my senior season I told myself I had to look at life like she did. I chose to seize every moment like it was my last, so that I could live my very best life.

Luckily—like Lizzie—I had a great team on my side, and they supported me when I was feeling terrible *and* when I was doing great. And, thankfully, Delaware won every single game in my absence, which took away a lot of my angst about missing them.

But one of our biggest games was coming up, and the last thing I wanted to do was sit it out.

On December 20, I still wasn't feeling great, but I decided I was well enough to get back on the court in a home game against our archrival, University of Maryland. We were on a four-game winning streak, but Maryland was ranked number nine in the country, and we hadn't beaten them in eleven outings. They'd also defeated us the previous year in our only regular-season loss, and we were desperate to avenge it. We knew we were playing better than we ever had, so we were prepared.

But was I?

You might be weak and skinnier than you've been in years, but you need this game. Seize this moment, I reminded myself.

I'm not sure if it was the fact that the matchup was just before Christmas, so everyone was ready to party, or if it was because Maryland games were always popular, but the Bob was packed that night.

"It's because you're back," one of my teammates joked, but I knew it wasn't only that. More than five thousand people—the largest crowd that had ever filled the Bob for a women's basketball game—wanted to see us beat our neighboring state and sworn enemy, and they came out cheering for us to do it.

The first half was a tight race. They'd score, and we'd answer. We'd sink a basket, and they'd rebound, taking the ball down the court, past our defenders, and right through the net. I struggled and even fell to the floor a few times, but without fail I forced myself up. *Just keep muscling,* I told myself.

We tied it up seven times as we raced to catch up with them, but Maryland was the best rebounding team in women's college basketball, and when we were inside the paint, it was always hard. I was still feeling weak, and a lot of the time their defense was just too much for me. When we'd put the pressure on them, they'd go on a run, like the six-point unanswered streak they had at the end of the first half, which put them up 35–28.

When the second half began, it was like they hadn't even needed a break. Maryland burst out of the gate, scoring eight points right away—all off rebounds. Like I said, they were the best in the country at doing just that! They built their lead to fourteen before I doubled my efforts, grabbed the ball, and in a few minutes sank three three-pointers. We'd narrowed down the Maryland lead to within three.

Unfortunately, right after that the game was all theirs. The Terrapins scored twelve straight points, we didn't make a basket for a full six minutes, and well over half of my shots from the field couldn't connect. When the game ended with a 69–53 victory for them, it was clear we just hadn't been up for the challenge.

"Today's game was about two teams who are in two very different places right now," Coach Martin said to the press.

I couldn't have agreed more. They were at the top of their game, and we were playing catch-up, especially with me sick. But as I always tell the kids I work with in basketball clinics, without mistakes you can't learn anything. We'd made plenty on the court that night, but we were poised to grow from them.

And grow we did. After the loss to Maryland, we won game after game, most by double digits. We had an overtime squeaker against St. John's University that ended 60–59, but other than that it was all Blue Hens, all the time. We won the CAA tournament easily, advancing us automatically into the NCAA tournament, where we were going to face West Virginia University on our home court.

Chapter Eighteen

Saying Good-bye

Ever since I was a kid, I've lived in my head—sometimes too much. When I refused to go to the mall with Mom before practice because it might make me too tired, I was over-thinking. When I chose to accept a scholarship to UConn even though my soul was screaming that it was a mistake, I was going with my head rather than my heart. Ever since I burned out, though, I've realized how important it is to trust how you're feeling. I've discovered I need to check in with my instincts, then follow them. Because nine times out of ten, my body and spirit are right.

Just before our first-round NCAA tournament matchup against West Virginia, I was feeling great. The year before, entering the tournament had seemed scary and new. We'd been the underdogs, right? So that had meant we had to be on our toes a little more. This year we felt like old pros. We were confident. We knew what we were getting into. *If you're feeling this way,* I told myself, *then act on it. Go out and win this game like a veteran.*

Unfortunately, our first half against West Virginia made

us look as inexperienced as we'd felt the year before. We tried a man-to-man defense that failed again and again, and our opponent finished up the second half with a 33–26 lead. In the locker room we decided to switch things up, going with a two-three zone formation that would make them rely on their outside shooting. *We're in front of a home crowd that is desperate for us to win,* I thought, *so we have to show them that we know how to do this. Because I know we do.*

In the second half we rallied. Our zone clicked into place, and we started getting offensive rebounds that we'd missed in the first half. Then we made them connect. We drew fouls, too—so many that I was sent to the line thirteen times after not getting there a single time in the first half. Feeling like the veteran I knew I was, I scored twenty points—half of the forty points we put on the board in the second part of the game. After wearing West Virginia down and watching their star player head to the sidelines after fouling out, we defeated them 66–53.

As you know, the Delaware women's team had never advanced beyond the second round of the tournament. Getting to the Sweet Sixteen is no easy feat—especially for a small conference team like us. But when it's your senior year and you know that it's your last chance to make history for a school that welcomed you with open arms in your darkest moments, you know you've got to do it.

Just before our game against the University of North Carolina, I thought back on how I'd felt during my sopho-more year, when I couldn't get out of bed. I had been in the dark, clueless about what was wrong with me, and I couldn't figure out why someone like me was being tested that way. Hadn't I been through enough? Or was this some kind of sick joke about me coming to grips with how much I missed basketball?

Well, I'd come back. But now it was time to really *prove* it. Sometimes surviving something awful isn't enough to make you feel victorious about what you've accomplished. You have to show that you can stomp all over the thing that set you back—then perform better than you ever have in your life.

That test would be our game against UNC.

It was my last home game at UD, and the stadium was packed—just like it had been for our matchup with West Virginia. But the energy was *different* this time. We were considered the underdog, so fans were pumped. Vice President Biden was there, so security was tight. Finally, sitting across the court from Sylvia Hatchell, whose scholarship offer I'd turned down years before, I couldn't help but think, *I wonder if she realizes how happy I am that I chose Delaware.*

The truth is that I was happy. In Delaware I'd found a community that embraced me even when I didn't want to play basketball. Most of them had been understanding when I got sick. They didn't think it was weird that I wanted to be close to my family. After a bad burnout I think it's important to find a comfortable, happy, and loving spot to feel safe, and they'd provided that for me. The fact that it was my last home game in a place that had been so wonderful to me almost made me cry.

But it's time to prove myself, I thought. *And we're going to win this game.*

Despite the electricity in the air and a crowd that kept screaming "Let's go, Hens!" the first half was terribly disappointing. We were down by five points six minutes in, and I had to limp to the sidelines—then back to the locker room—with a sore knee. After I returned, we scratched and clawed our way into the lead late in the half, but it didn't stick. By halftime we were down by eight points. We were feeling anxious even though I'd narrowed the lead from eleven with a last-second three-pointer.

The second half started even rockier. With sixteen minutes left in the game, we were down 48–39, and I think that's when, collectively, we decided to come alive. Now, I'm used to being the one to save a game. I can take charge, shouldering the burden of bringing a team back from the brink of losing. But one of the beautiful things about a team is that sometimes, when you least expect it, new leaders emerge.

That's what happened with my teammate Trumae Lucas. She charged, she scored sixteen points, and she stole the ball three times. She drew fouls right and left, and North Carolina got into foul trouble—big-time—as their two leading scorers went to the bench with four fouls each. We scored six straight points—including my three thousandth as a Blue Hen—and soon we were up 52–51. We kept the pressure on, and by the time the buzzer rang, we'd won 78–69.

The crowd went crazy. They'd been on their feet all day—including Vice President Biden, who was supposedly blocking everyone behind him—and as I walked out to the middle of the floor, I held back tears.

We made it to the Sweet Sixteen. After four years of loving this sport more and more every day, I've discovered something new: the feeling that if it all goes downhill from here, at least I knew what it was like to be on top.

The final rounds of the NCAA tournament are held in neutral locations, so we headed to Bridgeport, Connecticut, to play the University of Kentucky. It was a game none of us ever thought we'd reach, and a matchup we weren't expected to win.

We tried our hardest, but we just couldn't fend off Kentucky. By the half, we were down 21–17, and while we were used to trailing midway into the game, we felt drained by how difficult everything had been so far. At one point I'd scored ten points in a row, but my teammates had struggled throughout the game to get the ball in the bucket.

When the second half began, we tried our hardest to overtake them, but we couldn't get there. I thought we might. With 2:47 left, we scored to make it 62–60, but then Kentucky answered with a three-pointer, and the game was all theirs from that moment on. The final score was 69–62, and as the buzzer went off, I dropped my head and let the moment sink in.

It's okay, I thought. *We made it further than ever before, and that's a big victory.*

Right after the game was over, a reporter came up to me.

"You know that you're now the fifth-leading scorer in

NCAA history, right? You passed three players—Cheryl Miller, Chamique Holdsclaw, and Maya Moore—today when you hit three thousand and thirty-nine points."

"I had no idea," I said honestly. "It's incredible and humbling to be among those names."

It was. Sure, I'd decided when I was four that I wanted to be a basketball star, but the sport had become so many more things to me. It wasn't about winning or breaking records, and I couldn't have cared less about being famous. Basketball was about love: the love of my teammates, my town, my school, my coaches, and my family. But most of all, it was about me finally being passionate about the sport with all my heart.

It was a feeling I'd need to carry with me as I finished up my senior year and headed toward the WNBA draft.

PART THREE
FORWARD

Chapter Nineteen

WNBA Draft

UD had taught me so many things. Sure, academics had been a huge part of my time there—I'd studied with professors who were at the top of their field, and I'd been constantly challenged by my classes—but the most valuable lesson I'd learned was how to balance. In college I'd had to keep up my GPA, perform well at practice and games, and after hours work with developmentally challenged kids, which was required by my major. I was always running from the Bob to class to special education centers off campus, then trying to find a spare hour or two for my family and friends.

Trust me, figuring out how to manage being all over the place wasn't easy, but I knew it was an essential skill. After all, life is a *huge* balancing act, and after college my schedule was only going to get crazier. When I left UD and became a professional athlete, I'd be expected to train harder; play with more confidence in front of larger, more demanding crowds; and enter into endorsement deals that would make me and the sport more visible. My life would be all basketball, all the time—much more than it had been in college.

Luckily, UD had helped me realize that I couldn't let that single-minded focus consume me. School had taught me that you have to find something you're passionate about, then turn it into fun. As I headed toward the WNBA draft, I was determined that I wouldn't burn out, and I knew that balancing all my interests was the key to that.

Still, I was nervous. I'd run out of steam before, and the memory haunted me. So I kept reminding myself, *This is what you want to do. If you remember that, you'll enjoy it.*

The WNBA draft was set to happen on April 15, before my graduation. But the entire selection process had started back in September, when a lottery had determined which four WNBA teams—out of the twelve in the league—would get the first draft picks. Then, on April 11 the league would invite twelve women to attend the actual draft selection, which would be on prime-time TV for the first time ever. These twelve weren't the only players who'd be snatched up by the league, but they were the public faces of the incoming WNBA class, considered to be the best out there.

I was on that list, and I couldn't have been happier. But part of balancing involves managing your expectations and letting go, and in the four days before the draft, I had to do just that.

You need to stay steady, Elena, I told myself. *Sure, you're about to explode from excitement, but you're not going to be the top pick. You may not even be second—or third. Don't let that disappoint you. Don't put all your hopes into one team either. Just be happy wherever you end up.*

Brittney Griner from Baylor University was expected to

be the top pick. She was super-tall at 6'8", was the best shot blocker in the country, and had led Baylor to two national championships. During her junior year Baylor had a 40–0 season, something no team—ever—had done. Brittney was considered by almost everyone to be one of the best female college players in women's basketball history, and I didn't disagree. She was a legend, and any team would be lucky to have her.

Then there was Skylar Diggins, a powerhouse player from Notre Dame, whom I'd been on the World University Games team with back in college. Skylar was an NCAA leader in steals and assists and one of the top free throw scorers in the nation. She was also a social media star, which would bring thousands of new fans to whatever team chose her. I loved Skylar, but I wasn't sure I had half the charisma or charm that she did.

People were calling me, Brittney, and Skylar the "Three to See," and while we had a lot of similarities—especially that we were great all-around players—there were two big, glaring differences. First, I was the only one of them with a chronic illness. Every coach out there knew that a Lyme disease flare-up might cause me to miss games—and that was a big risk for them. Second, I'd left the number one college team in the nation without even telling the head coach. Could I be trusted?

You can't think about that, Elena, I told myself. *You are who you are, and your past is what it is. Just stay focused and balanced.*

The twelve women who'd be featured during the draft selection headed to Bristol, Connecticut, a few days before the big event. Mom and Dad planned to drive and meet me on the day of the draft, but I flew up, on pins and needles the whole time. It wasn't just because a huge, life-changing moment was about to happen either; I was secretly hoping that one particular team would pick me, but I couldn't tell anyone.

I really, really like the Chicago Sky, I said to myself. *I want them so much.*

The Sky had just barely missed the play-offs the year before, so I knew they were itching for a big point-scorer who could push them over the edge of greatness. I'd always thrived on that kind of challenge, and I could see exactly how and where I'd contribute on the court. Plus, my pre-draft interview with the coaches and owner had gone really well. Even though they'd asked me some hard questions, I loved that they weren't afraid to discuss my burnout.

"It's not going to happen again," I'd told them confidently. "I'll be fine. I promise you. I'm 100 percent committed."

I also felt comfortable discussing my health with them when they pressed me on it.

"I've gotten sick before, and I might miss games in the future, but I have my health under as much control as I can. I have great doctors who keep me on a daily regimen of medication and treatments, and we work *hard* to keep me healthy."

The team told me they'd have to look at medical records closely, but that didn't bother or surprise me. Doing a background check on a player's injuries or health history was totally routine. More than anything else, I appreciated that such an important organization was so honest with me. That kind of communication seemed like a good sign.

What *did* bug me a little, though, was that for the first time in my basketball career, I wasn't in control of where I'd play. When I'd accepted UConn's offer, I'd chosen them. When I'd left to go to UD, the decision had been all mine. Sure, I hadn't had a say in who my coaches or teammates were, but I'd been in charge of my future.

With the WNBA draft, though, I wasn't. Whichever team chose me would be the one my agent would begin negotiations with. Then I'd pack up my life, move, and start practicing with the team before the season started the following month. Everything was happening so quickly, and I felt like a wave had swept me up and was carrying me away from shore, far from my past and everything I knew.

Deep breaths, I told myself. *Just because you're not in control doesn't mean you can't feel balanced.*

I slept fitfully and woke up before dawn the day of the draft. The other top picks and I had *so* much to do that day: interviews, meetings, photo shoots, promotional events, and more. To prepare for them I had to get my hair and makeup done, change outfits at least three times, review and memorize TV scripts, and make sure I was on time to the bus that would take me around the ESPN studios. I wasn't a total TV newbie—I'd been filmed playing in high school and college and had done postgame interviews—but draft day was different. It was a prime-time celebrity event, and the butter-flies in my stomach were going crazy because of it.

Just before eight p.m., Brittney, Skylar, nine other women, and I walked into one of ESPN's brightly lit studios, sat in high-backed chairs facing a stage, and waited for the cameras to start rolling. My dad was on my right, and my mom was on my left, and before I even got comfortable, I heard a woman's voice booming through the studio as she welcomed everyone.

Then she moved on to business.

"For the first pick in the 2013 WNBA draft, the Phoenix Mercury choose . . . Brittney Griner!"

Like I said, Brittney's getting chosen first by Phoenix was hardly a surprise. She was so sure, she'd even painted her nails orange, their team color! She wasn't unfazed about being a guaranteed pick, though. As the audience started clapping and cheering, she stood up, broke out into a huge smile, and hugged the people she'd brought with her. Then she walked up to the stage to be photographed holding a Phoenix jersey, looking like the happiest person in the room.

The next team to pick would be the Chicago Sky. Their head coach, Pokey Chatman, worked with a team in Moscow in the WNBA off-season, so she had to announce her pick at six a.m. Russia time. Apparently she'd been up all night, and I imagined that she felt as worn-out as I did.

It's going to be Skylar, I thought. *I'm sure of it. She's from Indiana, so she's practically a hometown girl. Everyone loves her. She's an amazing player, and she's just what the Sky need. I know you want Chicago, Elena, but disappointments can be good for you. They help keep you grounded and your life balanced.*

Skylar wasn't the only thing worrying me, though. The team's questions about my Lyme disease kept coming back into my mind. I knew I had my health under control, but a flare-up *could* happen at any time, without notice. Was that too much of a risk for them?

The little voice in my head spoke up again. *It's the issue in your life that's most out of your control, which is why you have to let it go. There's nothing you can do.*

Suddenly I realized that having no control meant that everything—the good *and* the bad—was unexpected. And if something really great happens when you don't see it coming, that's the best surprise in the world!

I was on pins and needles, about to find out if that would happen to me.

Pokey had started talking, but none of us could hear her because the television monitor she was on was offstage. Instead the woman at the podium heard the name in her earpiece, and after she finished listening, she lowered her head to the mike.

"With the second pick in the 2013 WNBA draft, the Chicago Sky pick . . . Elena Delle Donne from the University of Delaware!"

I think people started clapping, but honestly, I'm not sure. I was too busy listening to the sound of my breath coming up from my lungs and out of my mouth. I'd been holding it for what felt like a minute. Then, as I pushed back my chair to stand, my mom and dad rose with me, and I hugged them tight.

This is one of the happiest moments of my life, I told myself. *It's what I wanted. It's what I've been working toward forever. But, wow, it's a lot to take in.*

I didn't realize it then, but I'd be feeling that way for a while.

Chapter Twenty

Moving to Chicago

When I was sitting in the ESPN studio, waiting to hear my name called, with my parents quietly sitting beside me, I felt like time was standing still. I heard Brittney's name, and I saw lights flashing, and then the silence that followed seemed to swallow me. My thoughts were focused on one thing: when my name would be called. I was living in a moment that was encased in three words: "Elena Delle Donne." And when I heard those words, it was like a balloon popped in my head.

Now things are happening. My life is moving forward, and it has swept me up fast.

I walked onto the stage to claim my Chicago Sky jersey and take photographs. Then I was ushered into a back room to do a few interviews. When I watch them now, I agree with everything I said, because it's absolutely how I felt at the time. I was thrilled to be chosen by Chicago. They were the team I'd wanted, and getting to play in the WNBA was a dream come true.

Plus, I was *so* ready—emotionally and physically. My brother, Gene, had been psyching me up for weeks, saying things like "We have to get you mentally tough. Let's do Kobe's workout." He even brought out boxing gloves during one practice session to prepare me for all the body contact I'd face in the WNBA.

Being ready doesn't mean you can't *feel* overwhelmed, though—especially when everyone around you is focusing on your future. Reporters were quizzing me on how I'd fit into the Sky, whether I thought I could take them to the play-offs for the first time in their history, and how I felt about moving away from Delaware, a place I'd lived my entire life. Every question being thrown my way was about a month from now, not the present, and it was starting to make my head spin. So I decided to pause for a moment and think about what joining the WNBA meant to me.

I need to appreciate what I've been given just for now. This is a huge second chance.

When I'd left UConn five years before, I'd thought basketball was over for me. But here I was now, at the top of the sport. In five years I'd learned and grown so much. I'd become a different person, and that was a true gift.

One thing I've learned since I burned out at UConn is that I'm not the only person who forgets to live in the moment. Far too many kids are taught that the future is all that they should think about. It's a target or goal to reach, and they have to practice, study, or prepare for it every hour of every day. That kind of thinking is toxic, and it ignores all that you do—and all that you can be proud of—in the moment. In my opinion, it's also a surefire recipe for burnout.

That's why I was allowing myself to close my eyes and be thankful, if only for a few seconds. When I opened my eyes, I faced the reporters' questions, and suddenly I felt 100 percent prepared to think and act on my future.

The beginning of the WNBA season was in May, and it was already mid-April. I'd officially graduated in the fall, but I was still taking classes—which was required for me to stay eligible for the draft—so I'd have to finish them and take my finals. Then I'd have to pack up my dorm room, pick and choose what I wanted to take from home to Chicago, find an apartment, move, and start practicing with the Sky. Our first game was May 25!

But, again, I was so thankful I'd gotten a second chance to play the sport I loved, so I told myself I should just roll with it. This was a decision I'd made, on my own terms and after years of consideration. I was prepared.

I was also flooded with emotion. Except for the two days I'd lived in Connecticut, I'd spent my entire life in Delaware, and it was home. I loved it with every bone in my body. I knew my parents and Gene would be able to fly anywhere to see my games, but Lizzie wasn't very mobile, and sitting in a crowded, smelly stadium for hours would be too disruptive for her. I had to accept that I'd be seeing her a lot less.

There was no way around it. Leaving her was going to break my heart. But if I wanted to continue to grow, and to do what I was sure, deep in my heart, was my life's calling, I had to accept that.

I cried when I hugged and kissed Lizzie good-bye, and I

cried when I boarded the plane to Chicago. When I moved into the apartment I'd found—the first place I'd live on my own, as a real grown-up—I missed her so much my heart hurt. But I knew I'd see her as soon as I got a break, and I'd make every moment count.

Because practice started right away, I had no time to soak up my surroundings, explore my neighborhood restaurants and shops, or even learn much about this brand-new place that was so much bigger than where I'd spent my life. Chicago was such a strange, foreign land that everything surprised me, even obvious stuff that now makes me laugh when I think about it.

For example, only a day or so after I arrived, I was riding in a car toward a preseason interview when I looked out the window and saw a massive body of water looming in the distance.

Wait, there's an ocean here? I thought, lost in wonder. Then I shook my head when I realized how silly I was being. *That's Lake Michigan, dummy. You just had no idea a lake could be so big.*

People were friendly and welcoming, though. My teammates, coaches, and the Sky organization seemed to want to take care of me and make me feel at home. With them on my side, being in a new place, far from my family, didn't feel as terrifying as it had when I'd gone to UConn, and I was excited in a way I hadn't expected. *Maybe this is easier because I'm growing up,* I thought. *I've come a long way in five years.*

It was also easy not to think too much about home because I was so busy. There was an incredible amount to do as we got ready for our first game against the Phoenix Mercury, a team that had as much to prove as we did.

Chapter Twenty-One

Toss Out Your Expectations and Make Goals

Expectations can be a terrible thing for a person. If you put them on yourself—for example, if you just expect that you'll get into a certain college because your grades and scores are so good—you might feel like a failure if you don't do so. If someone else puts them on you—say, your mom is certain that you'll get into the play you auditioned for—you might feel like you disappointed that person if you don't get the part. Much of the reason I burned out when I was eighteen was because I had so many expectations put on me, by myself and by too many people in my life. So when I was in college, I discovered a way to think of expectations a little differently.

Rather than calling them expectations, I started to imagine them as goals. Goals are hopes for the future. They're positive things that inspire you, not negative things that stress you out. "Goal" implies potential and big dreams, not scary things with crazy, impossible deadlines.

When I was drafted into the WNBA, I told interviewers that one of my goals for the year was to help get Chicago into the play-offs. They'd finished the previous season with a disappointing 14–20 record, which was the worst in the WNBA and so low that they knew midway through the season that they likely wouldn't make it to the postseason. Morale was still low from having that losing record the year before, but adding me—a top pick in the draft—injected some hope.

I was determined that I wouldn't buckle from the pressure. *No one is forcing you to push the Sky into the play-offs,* I told myself. *That would be crazy. It can't be all on you. But you can do everything possible to help make that happen. It's a goal you can work toward.*

I walked onto the court for my first game against the Phoenix Mercury already dreaming about the play-offs. Sure, it was only day one of the season, but there was no harm in me imagining the cheering crowds that would fill the stadium if the Sky got into the postseason. I knew I could live in the moment, focusing on winning this one game, and still be excited that our season might end on a huge high note. Having goals doesn't mean that you ignore the moment you're in. It just means that you savor it and still dream about something bigger and brighter.

As I said before, Chicago was coming off a losing season, but Phoenix's had been terribly disappointing too. They'd finished the previous year with a 7–27 record—the second worst in the WNBA. They needed dominant players, so they snatched up Brittney Griner in the draft. She wasn't the only big name there, though. Diana Taurasi, who'd been a superstar at UConn a few years before I got there and was one of the most celebrated women in WNBA history, had been with Phoenix since she'd gone pro in 2004.

Brittney and Diana were massive talents, and I'd be going head-to-head against them for the first time in my career. Was I nervous because of that? Sure. Who wouldn't be? But having a goal means that you have to face all the scary feelings that come with the possibility of success. I accepted the butterflies in my stomach, begged them to calm down just for a bit, and then stood with my teammates to walk onto the court, more excited than I'd ever been in my life.

First, though, I went through two of my tried-and-true pregame rituals.

For as long as I can remember, I've always bought a pack of gum before games. It's always the same brand: one of the Wrigley flavors. I go to the store, spend more time than I should staring at the packs of gum in the candy aisle, and then finally settle on the one that speaks to me. I can't explain what it is about the particular pack of gum I like. It might be the flavor or just where it's positioned in the row, but all I know is that I have to *feel* it.

No one is allowed to touch my gum, and if they do, I have to throw it out. I worry sometimes that I won't have time to buy a new pack, so I've started hiding it in my locker just to be safe. Then right before each game, I take out a piece, put it into my mouth, and begin to chew it. *Who knew good luck tasted like mint?* I might say to myself. If the game's going well, I'll keep chewing. But if we're losing by the half, I'll spit out my gum and start all over with a new piece.

My second pregame ritual will probably make more sense to you—and make me seem less crazy!

When I was twenty, I got a tattoo of Lizzie's name on my left rib cage. I chose that spot because I wanted the tattoo to be my little secret, like it was a special thing that made her truly a part of me. But the placement also makes sense, now that I think about it. Lizzie is right next to my heart all the time.

Lizzie couldn't be at my first WNBA game, which wasn't a surprise or at all unusual. But my dad was front and center in the stands, prepared to cheer me on the whole time. Since the game was in Phoenix, though, he was one of the only Chicago fans. The rest were all about the Mercury, and they were pumped—not just because it was the beginning of a season but also because Brittney Griner brought a special skill that few people ever see in a women's basketball game.

At 6'8", Brittney is one of the only WNBA players who dunk during a game. In the heat of play, most female players can't extend themselves high enough to reach a ten-foot basket. Candace Parker and Lisa Leslie have also dunked midgame, and I could, technically, but my vertical isn't even *close* to theirs. I've also never had the opportunity. I can only dunk if it's the start of the game, I'm super-fresh, and I have a clear path to the basket. Brittney, on the other hand, dunks like she could do it in her sleep. She did it all throughout college, and Phoenix fans were banking on the fact that she'd do it again during her first regular season appearance.

From the minute the whistle blew, the game was all ours. We made basket after basket, and I could tell right away that

Phoenix was getting frustrated. Forget dunking; our defense was so strong that Brittney could hardly get a shot in. We kept drawing fouls on her too, and by the end of the first quarter she was almost in foul trouble with three under her belt. Three more and she'd be out of the game. By the time the halftime buzzer rang, we'd allowed her to get only two points on the board, and we were up by twenty-four points.

No need for a second piece of gum, I thought. *Thank you, Lizzie!*

We dominated in the second half just as we had in the first. Even though Brittney got her much-anticipated dunk in in the fourth quarter (and it was one-handed!), and then again in the last minutes of the game (a two-hander!), we still won the game by a huge stretch. It was 102–80 when the buzzer rang.

It was amazing. There was no other way to put it. Even though I scored twenty-two points throughout the game—the sixth-best in a WNBA start—the game hadn't all been on my shoulders. Epiphanny Prince, who'd been playing professionally for three years, was the team leader with twenty-six points, and she rallied all of us toward the beautiful victory we had.

As I walked back into the locker room, dizzy from excitement, my head was exploding with all the possibilities that could happen in my first year playing professionally. After all, I had a goal to reach, and I knew that couldn't happen unless I started to think of basketball—and my life—differently than I ever had before.

Chapter Twenty-Two

Living and Playing Differently

By the end of the first ten games of my rookie season with the WNBA, I knew I was playing some of the best basketball of my life. I was dominating across the court, I was frequently the league leader in free throws, I was averaging almost twenty points a game, and during almost every game I had one or two blocks that helped turn the tide of play around. Chicago was 7–3 overall and undefeated at home, and the media was calling us the team to beat in 2013. What a difference that was from the year before!

I'd been on a lot of great teams in my life. Ursuline had won state championships, and UD had made it to the Sweet Sixteen, but in both of those cases I'd been playing with women around my age. In the WNBA, players were often older than me—some of them by six, seven, even eight years. These players were world famous, too. Look at Diana Taurasi, for example. I'd idolized her in high school!

On the Sky, I was practically the baby of the team. Swin Cash had been playing professionally for eleven years and had just gotten back from the Olympics; Sylvia Fowles had been with the Sky for five years; and Epiphanny Prince wasn't that much older than me, but she'd played in Europe for a year when I was still close to home in Delaware. She brought a worldview that I'd experienced only when I'd played in the World University Games.

I'm learning something from these veterans, I realized. *This is awesome.*

On the Chicago Sky, I had to adjust my style of play to the rhythm that these tried-and-true players had developed over years. I took their experience and applied it to my own, and we got better and better as a team. Suddenly I began to think of basketball differently. It wasn't just a sport or a game that was strictly in the moment. Instead it was like the buildings my dad built: the foundation might have been old, and some of the materials might have been recycled, but when it all came together, the structure was new.

These veterans weren't just going to teach me lessons on the court, either. Every WNBA game was televised, and after every single one, many of us would have to speak to reporters, so I was going to have to learn to be professional in front of the camera. Other than the media blitz surrounding the WNBA draft, this was pretty new to me, and I'd have to depend on my coaches and teammates to show me what to do.

Pokey was an old pro, though, and she had a plan.

"I know every reporter is going to want to talk to you about leaving UConn," she told me one day. "But we're not doing that. We're talking about you on *this* team."

Her words came as such a relief. It wasn't a lie not to discuss

UConn. I wasn't shedding my old life or burying something that had happened five years before. Just like my team, I was using it as my foundation, then building off it. I was making something entirely new that was going to carry me forward.

Pretty soon I decided to think of my life in Chicago that way too. Sure, I missed Delaware and Gene and Lizzie and all the friends I'd known and loved since I was a kid, and I spent way too many nights on the phone with them, sometimes in tears. But I'd made a decision to be in Chicago, I'd signed a contract, and I was on a team that was taking me places I'd never been before.

For the entire season, your life is here, I told myself. *You need to let this city teach you something. You're the rookie, and it's the veteran.*

With that attitude, I put my trust in the security of my new situation and decided to make myself feel really at home. I didn't just go furniture shopping or throw a housewarming party either. I decided to look for a dog.

My family had always owned Great Danes, and I absolutely loved the breed. Our first was Raider, whom Mom had found when she was on a run when I was five, and later we owned our beloved Champ. It had been five years since he'd died, and I still missed him. Great Danes reminded me of Mom and Dad and my happy childhood, and they were tall and all legs just like me, so I couldn't imagine any breed who'd make me feel more at home.

After days of looking online, I found the perfect pup. I contacted the breeder in Iowa, I made the adoption official, and she drove him to me. He was a beautiful, floppy-eared, slobbery male with the most gorgeous blue eyes I'd ever seen, and I loved him from the moment he wiggled in my arms.

The problem was that I wasn't sure what to call him. I came up with a few names, but I hated all of them after a few hours. This beautiful puppy went without a name for two straight weeks until the night that I threw out the first pitch at a Cubs' game, and a thought struck me.

I'll name him Wrigley. It's the perfect name for a Chicago dog.

I loved taking my big guy for walks. Everyone would comment about his massive paws, and his beautiful gray coat, and how they couldn't believe that such a tall person would buy what was soon going to be a huge dog.

"What's his name?" they'd ask.

"Wrigley," I'd answer.

"Oh, really? My neighbor's dog is named Wrigley. So's my niece's."

Here I was, thinking I was so original by calling him Wrigley. Yet half the dogs in Chicago apparently had the same name.

Even though in name he wasn't half as unique as I'd dreamed he'd be, Wrigley became my best friend, and we went everywhere together. But I started to make other (human) friends too.

Most of the people I began meeting were somehow connected to the Sky, so while we had basketball in common, we all came from different backgrounds. This felt so new to me, and pretty soon I realized that making friends wasn't about going to the same school or being from the same town. It was about finding something to talk about that you both liked, and then developing a connection from there.

My best friend, Meghan, and I were driving around one random night, searching for something to do. I'd just come from practice and hadn't had time to shower, so I looked like a mess. I'd thrown on my rattiest, ugliest hoodie, whose tie strings ended in little headphones rather than knots. I think I'd bought the hoodie as a joke, or maybe it had been on sale for 90 percent off, but I promise you it was *not* the kind of thing I'd ever wear out. So when Meghan suggested we meet a friend of hers for dinner, I was hesitant.

"I look like a wreck," I said. "This sweatshirt is ridiculous."

"You look fine," she laughed. "Besides, I want you to meet my friend Amanda. I think you two would get along."

Meghan had met Amanda a few weeks before at one of my games, and they'd become friends right away. I didn't know it at the time, but Meghan was positive that Amanda was perfect for me. She thought Amanda was just the person to challenge me and push all of my buttons—in a good way, of course! I trusted Meghan completely, so I finally said yes.

"Whatever," I said. "Let's meet your friend. I guess I have to eat, so why not do it with other people?"

Meghan called Amanda and arranged for her and her friend Leigh to meet us at a spot in our neighborhood. When we walked in and sat with them at our table, something about Amanda grabbed my attention. She was blond, like me. She'd played basketball in college. Me too. And she had this infectious smile that put me at ease right away. *I feel like I know her, and I haven't even talked to her yet.*

Pretty soon we started up a conversation, and it was just as natural as I'd hoped.

"I grew up in Rock Island, Illinois, on the Iowa border," she told me. "Then I went to Illinois State and was a point guard. Now I live here with my black Lab, Rasta."

"That's like me." I smiled, then corrected myself. "I mean, I have a Great Dane, not a Lab, and I haven't lived in Illinois all my life. I meant Delaware. Being here is the only time I've lived away from home."

"How do you like it?" she asked, then laughed and added, "Nice hoodie."

I broke out laughing. *She's gutsy,* I thought. Then I sat and thought for a moment or two. I liked Amanda. I *really* liked her, and I didn't want to say anything that wasn't totally honest. But the answer that came into my head was completely true.

"It's great," I said. "It's starting to feel like home. I'm happy here in a way I never expected."

What I couldn't tell her was what I was thinking deep down: I'd be a whole lot happier if I got to spend more time with her.

Chapter Twenty-Three

Rest, Refocus, and Rediscover Your Passion

The WNBA All-Star Game was set for July 27, 2013, and by the time it rolled around, the Chicago Sky was the best team in the Eastern Conference. Our record was 12–5, and we'd worked hard for every victory.

Being in the spotlight had never meant much to me, but I always appreciated fan support. Fans didn't care if you were famous or not; they just liked the way you played, and that was all the recognition I needed. Besides, the word "celebrity" or "star" felt fleeting, or like too much pressure. After my burnout, I couldn't take that. I wanted to play basketball, and play it well—not be some big shot who did it for the applause.

Fans voted on the players who would start in the All-Star Game, and they'd pick three frontcourt players and two guards. I knew I was a fan favorite based on how many little girls were lining up to meet me after games, but I had no idea just how popular I was. I got the most votes out of any WNBA player—35,656—and was the first rookie ever to come in first place in voting.

Unfortunately, though, I never made it to the All-Star

Game. In a matchup against the Washington Mystics, just three days before the All-Star Game was to be held, I got a concussion. In the last minute of the third quarter, a ball came loose, I scrambled for it at the same time as one of my opponents, and my head hit either the court or her knee. In an instant, I felt searing pain and saw a flash of light, and as I gripped the side of my head, I knew something wasn't right.

"Pokey," I said as I limped to the sidelines, "I need to get this checked out." I didn't tell her, but I knew I was out of the game.

After I was helped off the court by one of our trainers, doctors examined me, and they confirmed exactly what I was feeling.

"We're pretty sure it's a concussion, so we need to run some more tests. You need to sit on the bench the rest of the game, though."

I made my way back to the sidelines and watched my team lose, 82–78. When I went in for more tests that night, I got the news I was dreading: it *was* a concussion. The WNBA mandated that any player with a concussion would need to take time off and pass a few tests to make sure they were healthy enough to play, so I knew I'd be out at least four to five days. I'd miss the All-Star Game, and I might even be out longer than that.

Every player, in any sport, gets injured. It's one of the many risks you take when you play as hard as we do, and it's something you just have to live with. You're rarely alone on the sidelines either. Brittney Griner had just suffered a sprained left knee, and it had already been decided that she'd be missing the All-Star Game.

The pressure is so high when you're an athlete that you can't let the unavoidable make you crazy. If I'd gotten overly disappointed about my Lyme disease, my concussion, or the mono I got when I was in high school, I would have exploded from stress. That's why when the doctors gave me the bad news, I was frustrated and nothing more. My injury was going to disrupt the momentum of a great season, but there wasn't anything I could do.

When you have a setback like an injury, or you can't follow your passion because of something that there was no way you could have prevented, you just have to make the most of the situation. If you don't, you'll burn out. That's why I decided to go home to Delaware to rest up, see my family, and try to heal. I was there for almost a week, and I missed two games, plus the All-Star Game.

Unavoidable time off is also a great way to refocus on your priorities and passions. In Delaware I had the time and space to remember why I did what I did. I played basketball because I loved it—not because it was what I was supposed to do or because someone had told me to. I was in the WNBA because of true, honest passion for the sport. It had taken me places I'd never expected to go, tested me in ways that had taught me so much, and had given me goals that I couldn't wait to reach.

Being home also let me think about my relationship with Amanda. After our first dinner out with friends, she and I had traded numbers and promised we'd text each other to meet up again. At the time, I didn't know what would come of seeing her more. I was definitely attracted to her, but I'd have been just as happy having a new friend as I would a girlfriend, since my schedule was crazy. Finally I decided I didn't want to think *too* far ahead, so I told myself to let whatever was going to happen, happen, and be happy with it no matter what.

A few days after our first dinner, my phone made that familiar tri-tone sound, and I pulled it out to see who'd texted me.

> Hey, it's Amanda. It's beautiful out! U want to
> meet up at Montrose dog beach?

I texted back right away. Forget trying to play cool! Amanda had already seen me at my worst in that awful hoodie.

> Yeah! I can be there in an hour. I'm the tall girl
> with the huge dog.☺
> Great. I'll be there with Rasta.

For those of you who don't know Chicago, Montrose Dog Beach is a fenced-off area right on the shores of Lake Michigan just north of Wrigley Field. Dogs are free to dig in the sand, swim in the lake, and frolic to their hearts' content, and everyone always has a great time until a dog bypasses the fence and starts to bother the sunbathers on the "real people" side of the beach. I thought it was so cool that Chicago had a beach just for dogs and their owners, and the fact that Amanda had suggested going there made me like her even more.

She arrived right after I did. Rasta and Wrigley eyed each other cautiously, and then Wrigley walked toward Rasta to give him an approving sniff. Amanda and I took our shoes off, let the dogs off their leashes so they could run to the water, and then walked along the shore, laughing as they splashed around.

We could have stayed on that beach all day. The sun was shining gloriously, our dogs had become instant best friends, and we talked about everything from our families to basketball to what we wanted out of our lives. It was one of the best days I'd ever had, and Amanda and I didn't have to discuss what we both just *knew*. We were meant to be together.

When I was back in Delaware recovering from my concussion, I thought a lot about that day and all the times I'd had with Amanda since then. Without practice and travel and all the million other things that kept me way too busy, I took the time to thank the world for bringing her into my life. Then I flew back to Chicago on August 6, healthy, hopeful, and ready to help my team reach the goal I'd set for myself: to make the WNBA play-offs.

We did. In fact, the rest of my rookie season was everything I'd hoped for. In August we went 9–3, clinched the Eastern Conference title, and secured a spot in the WNBA play-offs. We'd be up against the Indiana Fever starting September 6, and to say we were excited would be the understatement of the year.

But first I'd have to come to grips with one of the most painful losses of my life.

Chapter Twenty-Four

Making Sense of Loss

One of my closest friends at home was named Mary Lacey. Our moms were best friends, and I'd known Mary Lacey pretty much since I was born.

I was such a serious kid in elementary school, but never with Mary Lacey. We played together; we laughed till we cried; and we loved running through our yards, making up whatever silly game our hearts desired. But in high school Mary Lacey started to struggle. We all had our issues with our bodies, dating, grades, or parents, but Mary Lacey took it all harder than most people. In college an even darker cloud descended on her, and I started to realize that maybe Mary Lacey's problems *weren't* just about the circumstances in her life. She was struggling from severe depression.

Just before the play-offs were set to begin, when I was still in Chicago training and getting ready, my phone rang. It was Gene.

"Elena," he said, his voice cracking, "I need to tell you something."

Gene is pretty much never super-serious, so hearing him

sound like that terrified me. "What is it? Is something wrong?" I was starting to get frantic.

"I'm so sorry, but Mary Lacey committed suicide."

I dropped my phone and burst into tears. I was over-whelmed with shock and sadness, and I couldn't believe that what Gene had said was real. *She couldn't have,* I thought. *She's my oldest friend. I love her too much.*

I must have sat on the couch for ten minutes before I realized I needed to call my mom. When she answered, I could tell she was sobbing.

"I'm driving to see Mary Lacey's mom," she said.

"Mom," I cried, "don't drive if you're like this. Go to Dad's office. Or pull over and I'll call him. I just don't want you to get hurt."

Mom has always been a rock, and hearing her this out of it was almost too much for me. Then it hit me: if Mom was that devastated, it was real. Mary Lacey was truly gone.

I managed to pull myself together enough to hear Mom say that I was right, and that she was going to find my dad.

"He'll drive me," she said. Then she started to cry all over again. "Oh, Elena. Mary Lacey was like my own daughter. If anything happened to you, Gene, or Lizzie, I just don't think I could go on."

Even though my head was swimming, I knew that wasn't true. "You would and you will, Mom. You're so strong. I love you. Please give Mary Lacey's mom all my love."

When we hung up, I went back to the couch and crawled

into a ball. *I know she'll make it,* I cried to myself. *She's my mom, and she's my hero. But the question is, what will I make of this? How can I ever find any meaning in something this awful?*

After a death, most people feel this way. We often wonder why someone so young and beautiful could die, and we start to worry that we'll never find happiness in anything ever again. The truth is that terrible things in life happen, but we *have* to keep moving forward. The future will offer you so many good things, and you need to be awake and aware enough to enjoy them.

It's totally understandable, though, for you to feel like whatever good things come your way are meaningless. After all, if the person we loved so much doesn't get to have them, what does any of it matter?

Sometimes it's not a question you can explore all by yourself. Luckily, I had Amanda to help me, and she couldn't have been more understanding and comforting if she'd tried. She encouraged me to mourn but not to lose sight of the fact that I could and should keep going. After all, I had a great life, a family who loved me unconditionally, and I was most likely about to be given one of the WNBA's biggest honors.

Just before the play-offs were set to begin, the league would be presenting one of the first-year players the Rookie of the Year Award. The media had been buzzing for weeks that I was the top contender, but I honestly didn't know how I felt about it. In fact, a big part of me didn't even want it.

I know I've worked for this, I thought, *but how can I be happy about it if Mary Lacey's not here?*

Then I remembered how I'd dealt with my whole first year in the WNBA: I'd thought about it differently. Not just that; I'd started to imagine my life in a whole new way, and that involved changing my attitude about death, too. I told myself that Mary Lacey might not have been around for me to thank her, but my team was. I would use the award to honor them, taking away the guilt I felt by making the prize a gift to others.

Just before our September 20 opening game against the Indiana Fever, Laurel J. Richie, the president of the WNBA, stood at a podium in front of my family, coaches, and a room full of media, and announced that all thirty-nine people who'd cast ballots for the Rookie of the Year Award had voted for me. As she pulled me into a big hug, I wasn't as shy or unhappy as I had thought I would be. I was thrilled, in fact, and most of all, honored.

But I needed to thank the people who'd made it happen, and they included Sylvia Fowles, who'd been named the Defensive Player of the Year, and Swin Cash, who'd tied for the Kim Perrot Sportsmanship Award.

"Truthfully," I said when I leaned down into the mike, "I talk about them because the individual accolades and the individual success doesn't come without them. They've helped me rise to the occasion game after game, practice after practice. So I'll continue to talk about them, because I owe them a ton."

Those words would ring in my ears throughout the play-offs. I'd need to remember how important my teammates were to me, because I was about to face one of the toughest challenges of my basketball career, against the Fever.

Chapter Twenty-Five

WNBA Play-offs

The first round of the WNBA play-offs consisted of only three games. That meant that every second counted, because if we went down one game, *everything* would ride on a second. There was no room for big mistakes to be made, and before we went into the play-offs against the Fever, we vowed that we'd try as hard as possible to avoid errors. Unfortunately, all the good intentions in the world don't guarantee that you won't slip sometimes. That's exactly what happened in our two games against Indiana.

Indiana was the defending WNBA champs, so seven of their veterans went into each game understanding the kind of pressure that goes into being in the play-offs. It was all new to the Sky, though. In eight years of franchise history, we'd never been to the play-offs.

Swin Cash later insisted that lack of experience had nothing to do with how we played, though. "The play-offs are about toughness, mental toughness, not about age," she said to the press.

If that was the case, then we just weren't tough enough. In

fact, we struggled mentally, physically, and emotionally from moment one.

Over the course of both games, the Fever out-rebounded us 70–51, even though we'd been the number two rebounding team in the nation all season. They nearly killed us on offense, too. During the first game, I made only ten points, which was less than I'd scored in all but one game during the regular season. My season average had been almost double that!

We lost the first game 57–79.

If every victory is a team effort, then every loss is as well, and my teammates had struggled as much as I had.

Sylvia Fowles got in fewer than 50 percent of her shots close to the net. Our point guard, Courtney Vandersloot, hardly completed any assists. We were four for seventeen on three-pointers, too. All around, we were outhustled, and we struggled over and over with our shooting and defense.

When the buzzer rang after the last game, which we lost 72–85, Courtney Vandersloot sat on the sidelines with her head underneath a towel and didn't move for several minutes.

I know how she feels, I thought. *I just want to hide too.*

But if you're ever going to come back from a devastating loss, you can't just disappear. Maybe you can squirrel yourself away for a few minutes, but soon you have to pick yourself up, dust yourself off, and learn something from it.

After the devastating 2013 play-offs, that's exactly what I planned to do.

Chapter Twenty-Six

Building Strength

I mentioned before that one of the things I always tell participants in the Elena Delle Donne Academy is that everyone is going to make mistakes, but that doesn't mean you're a failure. Quite the opposite, in fact; errors are a sign that you're only human, and if you don't make them, you won't learn anything.

When you're burning from a crushing loss, it's easy to lose sight of that. Failing hurts. You feel shame, anger, sadness, and even hopelessness, knowing that whatever you do next is going to be an uphill battle. But you have to keep trying— even if you can't figure out what you need to do. After all, haven't you *always* tried your best?

Before the play-offs, I definitely felt that way. I trained as hard as anyone I knew. I worked out four and a half hours a day with weights, on the court, and by running to build up my speed and stamina. It paid off too. All throughout high school and college, I was always at the top of my game from beginning to end. I didn't falter in the beginning of a game, then gain speed, and I certainly never sputtered out toward the end. The sum total of a game might have been a challenge, but I always thrived—and then some.

At some point during my rookie season with the Sky, though, that changed. I started to notice that I wasn't feeling as good in the second half of a game as I was in the first. I began to run more slowly, breathe more heavily, miss more shots, and go after the ball with less gusto than I had before. I wasn't sick or injured either. I just lacked the endurance I needed to take me through the end of a game as well as I'd started in the beginning.

Never had I been more aware of that than after our final loss to the Fever.

I could have felt better after halftime, I said to myself. *I was rested up, yet I was so slow.*

What could that be from? If I was already doing everything possible, what else could be causing it? It wasn't Lyme disease, so was I just getting old?

As the team was walking toward our press conference, where we'd have to recount not just how Indiana had swept us but also account for what we could have done better, I suddenly figured it out. I turned and grabbed Pokey by the arm.

"I don't think I'm strong enough, Pokey," I said to her as we rounded the corner toward the press room. "I think that's why I struggled so much in the second half of both games. I need to hire a strength coach in the off-season."

Pokey had been a coach for years, so she'd heard players say all kinds of things after big losses. Since she was someone whose job it was to help her team perform better and win games, I guess I thought she'd agree with me. What I didn't expect was that she'd tell me I was being too hard on myself.

"Elena," she said, almost like she was scolding me, "you are the Rookie of the Year. You had one of the best years I've ever seen from a new player. Can't you just stop and be thankful for that for a minute or two? Then we can figure out why we lost these games."

"Okay," I answered, half in shock and totally confused. *Isn't she happy that I want to improve?* I wondered.

"Look, I'm not disagreeing with you," she continued, probably noticing the weird look on my face. "But just think about this moment for right now. You just finished your season. Focus on that and speaking to the press. When we leave this room, we can think about next year."

And with that, we opened the doors, saw flashing bulbs, and began talking about the best season—and the worst end to it—that the Sky had ever had.

WNBA players aren't paid much compared to other professional athletes. On average we earn about $75,000 a year, and the best, most experienced player isn't allowed to make more than $109,000, a cap based on an agreement between the players and the league. NBA players have it *a lot* better. LeBron James is paid more than $30 million a year by the Cleveland Cavaliers. Think about that. He earns in one day what most female players do in a year.

The lower pay is why most WNBA players go overseas in the off-season to play for Russia, China, Turkey, Korea, Italy, or a handful of other countries. Players can make more than a million dollars on those teams! It's usually a fraction of what they'd make if they were men, but it's still great money. Unfortunately, traveling to another country means you're away from your family for months—unless they come with you. Maybe that might have been an option for my parents, Gene, or Amanda, but Lizzie couldn't do that. She could hardly leave the state of Delaware.

I'd thought a lot about what I wanted to do in the off-season, and I'd considered playing on a foreign team. Life in Chicago was expensive. I had endorsement deals, but making more money is always nice. Plus, the top players were almost *expected* to play overseas. It helped you keep your game up, raised your exposure internationally—which ultimately benefitted the WNBA—and taught you skills that only inter-national players could offer. The basic rules of basketball may be the same from country to country, but the style of play may not be, and I knew that I might come back from overseas with some really great tricks up my sleeve.

But I wouldn't see Lizzie for months, and the thought of that broke my heart.

I decided to turn down all the overseas offers and stay in Chicago over the winter. I could continue to take Wrigley on long walks, I could see Amanda as much as possible, and I could go home every weekend to see Lizzie. I'd also have time to do what I hadn't during the season: volunteer with special-needs kids and raise money for Lyme disease. I'd recently started working with the Lyme Research Alliance and the

Special Olympics, and the thought of devoting my energy to them was thrilling. In fact, I'd been named a global ambassador for the Special Olympics the year before, and it had been one of the prouder moments of my life.

The winter wouldn't be all fun and relaxation, though, because I planned to hire two people to help me build strength, and I wanted them to push me to the limit. Luckily, I found the perfect partners right in front of me. The first was one of Chicago's assistant coaches, Christie Sides, who would practice on the court with me and be my lifting buddy in the gym. The second was the Sky's strength coach, Ann Crosby, who would formally train me in all my lifting and conditioning.

For six months, till the Sky began practicing for the 2014 season, I'd meet Christie and Ann bright and early every morning for training. For the next four and a half hours, we'd stretch and lift weights, and then hit the court for drills. I'd worked out plenty in my life, but this was at a whole new level. I'd never pushed myself as hard or sweated as much as I did with them.

"I hate this," I told Christie every single morning in the beginning. "I feel terrible, and I'm not performing well because of it."

She was so reassuring. "Your muscles aren't used to it. Just keep at it, and soon they will be."

Within a few weeks I could tell a difference. I'd started putting on weight, and it was all muscle.

One of my favorite shots on the court is called a fade-away, which involves me jumping or leaning back just a bit to get away from a defender. I'm so tall that when I go for a fadeaway, then shoot, the ball is almost impossible to block. Defenders just can't get into the air fast enough, nor are they close enough.

"Forget fadeaways," Christie said one morning. "You've got to know how to make a shot when there's contact."

She was right. All during the previous season when a defender hit or touched me, I'd stumble out of position, and half the time miss the shot. Other times I'd just fall onto the court.

It's true, I thought. *I hate contact. I got a* concussion *from contact!*

Christie started intentionally fouling me—hard—and slowly I got comfortable with being bumped up against. As I put on muscle, the hits hurt less, and I didn't mind driving harder, risking knocking up against her. My body was responding in ways I'd never expected it to, and it was exciting.

This is so funny, I realized one day. *For years people have been worrying about my mental game. Like whether I'd burn out or run away because I wasn't happy. All that time I was ignoring the fact that my body needed to grow as much as my mind.*

I wasn't just building muscle and endurance during those months off. I was also working hard to keep Lyme disease from attacking, and I saw Rita Rhoads every other month for infusions of vitamin C. During one visit she noticed a difference in me right away.

"You seem healthy, Elena," she said. "That's great. I think you're going to have a fantastic season."

By the time the season was set to begin in May, I'd packed on twelve pounds of muscle, and I felt like a new woman. I could even do a pull-up—something I'd never before done because my wingspan is so huge.

I thought I was practically unbeatable, and I knew that no defensive player could knock me off my feet. Neither could Lyme disease, if I was lucky.

Unfortunately, I was only half right.

Chapter Twenty-Seven

Lead with Confidence

The word that sums up the beginning of the 2014 WNBA season for me is "confidence." The veterans, like me, had learned so much from the play-off sweep the year before, and we'd grown because of our mistakes and shortcomings. I'd grown too—literally! I was noticeably bigger and stronger, and just looking more athletic made me feel like I could do anything. Our rookies were also eager and had been terrific in practice, and they felt even more confident because they were working with players—like me and Sylvia—who'd been recognized and honored by the league. We were ready to tackle anything and anyone because we knew we were the team to beat.

Then Sylvia Fowles aggravated an old tissue injury in her hip and had to have surgery, and we were suddenly without our best defensive player. Christie had encouraged me to read books about leadership during the off-season, and thinking about them, I remembered a lesson I'd learned in college.

You've been a vocal leader before, and you can do it again. You're in a position to inspire this team, so do it.

During one practice just before the season began, I called the team together in a huddle.

"Listen," I said confidently, "we don't have Sylvia, and that's a big loss. But we have each other, and we're not the kind of team that depends on one player to do everything. We might play differently without her, but that doesn't mean we'll play worse. I'm confident we can be just as good as ever—even better. Are you?"

"Absolutely!" one person said.

Then another chimed in, "We can do this!"

Sure enough, we did. We had the best opening in franchise history, winning our first four games decisively. I captured the Eastern Conference Player of the Month for May, and Courtney Vandersloot had a career milestone when she became the Sky's all-time leader in assists.

Even without one of our best players, we're amazing, I thought. *Being confident has helped us so much.*

Unfortunately, confidence doesn't prevent bad things from happening. Just because you're feeling great doesn't mean that great things will happen, so I always think it's best to expect anything—good or bad—but always hope for the best. Lead with confidence, but know that reality can sometimes be ugly.

That's what happened during our eighth matchup, an away game against the Atlanta Dream.

I started to feel sluggish before I even got to the Atlanta stadium. We'd had a home game the day before, and the flight down had left me spent. I couldn't believe how tired I was even though I napped almost the whole trip, and when we landed, I felt like I walked off the plane in slow motion.

Now, I'd been fighting Lyme disease for five years, so you'd think I'd know right away when symptoms hit me. But since no flare-up is the same as the one before, this time I was pretty sure it was something else.

"I think I'm just overtired," I told Pokey. "I'm sure that getting on the court is going to energize me. I just know it."

It did exactly the opposite. During a time-out my hands were shaking so badly I could hardly hold my cup of water and drink it. I managed to play for only twenty-five minutes, and by the time I sat down on the bench, completely exhausted, I'd scored only seven points. We lost the game 59–97, our biggest defeat in terms of points all year.

I missed the next game, and the next four after that. When I finally got a proper diagnosis, I realized Lyme disease had been my problem all along. It had just been blossoming during the Atlanta game, preparing for a full-scale attack.

The previous two times Lyme disease had sidelined me, my symptoms had been like a bad case of the flu. My muscles and joints ached, and all I wanted to do was lie in bed. I also had brain fog, but it didn't stop me from being aware of my surroundings and making good decisions. This time was different. The fuzziness in my head got so bad that sometimes I didn't know where I was, and I couldn't figure out the simplest things, like what to eat for breakfast. I started having tremors, especially in my hands, and they got worse when I tried to practice. Can you imagine attempting a basket when you're not even sure you can hold on to the ball?

For a brief few days I started to feel better, so I played in one away game in Connecticut, but then I felt terrible. *Playing is just not worth the effort,* I realized, so I went home to Delaware and decided to see Rita daily for IV injections of antibiotics and vitamin C. I drove to her every morning, then spent all day in her office with needles and tubes in my arms.

Sounds like a really glamorous life for a basketball star, right? It was awful. Luckily, Amanda drove all the way from Chicago to Delaware with Wrigley in her car, then stayed with me in Delaware to take care of me and lift my spirits.

I tried as hard as I could to be optimistic, but the truth was, I was totally down in the dumps. I couldn't stop worrying that all the hard work I'd put in during the off-season had been for nothing. My muscles were withering away, I knew I'd have to spend at least six months getting my endurance back, and pull-ups? Forget it. The *thought* of doing one wore me out.

Worse, the Sky had gone 5–12 since I'd been home. It wasn't entirely because of me—Sylvia was still recovering from surgery, and Courtney Vandersloot had just been sidelined because of a knee injury—but I still felt awful. I hated seeing my team lose.

We're better than this, I thought. *And we were so confident!*

It's unrealistic to think that you won't feel depressed or angry when you're not at your best. It's okay to be frustrated— even desperate—when something that you've put months or years of your life into just disappears. I think you *have* to feel those emotions. Explore them. Even embrace them. Just know that they won't last forever, because chances are you're going to get better and learn from your experience. You may even come back with *more* confidence because you've been through so much.

. I don't regret a minute I spent recovering at home during the summer of 2014. I saw my family. I took walks with Lizzie. I got lots and lots of sleep. I learned to listen to my body, and finally I slowly started to feel better. My progress wasn't steady—I'd have good days, then bad days—but by the end of July, I could tell things were looking up.

Most of all, during my time away I discovered a love of basketball deeper than I'd ever known. I was so excited to play again that I could almost taste it.

I knew not to push myself, though. I'd learned a hard lesson in the game against Atlanta, and I accepted that I might play for only a few minutes during my first game back.

That's okay, I told myself. *If it's what my body needs, it's what I'll give it.*

On Thursday, July 31, I returned to Chicago, and I played for only ten minutes. But I scored ten points, and we beat the New York Liberty 87–74.

I might not have been at 100 percent, but I was back, still leading with confidence and a love of the game. That was all that mattered.

Chapter Twenty-Eight

Attitude Is Everything

Even though our season had had more highs and lows than almost any other team in the WNBA, by early August we still had a chance to make the play-offs. While I was out, Pokey had experimented with different configurations and new lineups, and players who'd never expected to start had helped see the bulk of the season through. When the injured players returned, many of these women went back on the bench, but their morale was high. They'd played confidently under incredibly trying conditions, and that had carried our team.

I'm not sure if it was that confidence that helped us wrap up our season as well as we did, but we went 5–3 in our final games and just barely snatched up the last spot in the Eastern Conference play-offs.

As we prepared for our series against the Atlanta Dream, I thought back on how I'd felt going into the play-offs the year before, when our situation had been so different.

We were number one in the conference then, I remembered. *Now we're the underdogs.*

For just a moment I got worried. If no one thought we'd win, did that mean we should be less confident? Should we just *expect* to lose, so when we did—if we did—we wouldn't be disappointed?

Never, I thought. *We can't think that way.*

In any situation, no matter how unlikely your chance of success is, I don't believe you can think negatively. Your confident attitude might just determine the outcome. After all, if you feel strong, you'll probably act that way. So while our future was totally unexpected, I chose to think of the unknown as exciting, not scary. It was an opportunity, and if something great happened in the play-offs, we'd be thrilled.

The Atlanta Dream had been swept in the WNBA finals the year before, and it still bothered them. That's why they headed into the play-offs feeling bullish. They had a brand-new coach, Michael Cooper, who'd energized them all year, and they walked onto the court in Atlanta wanting to win the semifinals probably more than any other team out there. They had something to prove, especially after losing ten of their last fourteen games.

I won't lie to you; I wasn't sure we could beat them. The beginning of the game sure made it seem unlikely too.

For the first quarter, we struggled, and we were down 17–30 when the clock ran out. Things didn't get much better in the second quarter either, and we were always behind by double digits. At the end of the first half, the score was 41–54.

The tide started to turn midway through the fourth quarter, though. With a pair of successful free throws, I narrowed Atlanta's lead to nine. Then we capitalized on fouls and turnovers and squeezed their lead to five. Then it was two. Atlanta stole the ball from me in a breathtaking move, and I couldn't catch up when they ran it down the court and brought the score within four.

Maybe because of Atlanta's speed and scoring ability in the first three quarters, we weren't expected to come back. Or maybe Atlanta was just too exhausted and too hyped up to keep the level of energy they'd maintained for almost a full forty minutes of play. All I know is that sometimes when you think positive and feel confident—and, most of all, remain open-minded about whatever might happen—you become tougher and gutsier than you've ever been.

And sometimes your opponent starts making mistakes.

With seventeen seconds left and a one-point lead, Atlanta missed two free throws. Then with 8.2 seconds left, I made a successful layup, and we were up by one point.

I don't remember exactly what I said in the huddle when a time-out was called. I know I tapped into all the things I'd learned about leadership during the off-season and didn't stand there silently. I yelled. I rallied. I pushed and became the positive, vocal force I'd learned how to be. And when we returned to the court for the last seconds of play, I didn't know what would happen, but I felt confident we could win.

As the clock ticked down, Atlanta took possession, moved

as close to the net as we'd let them, shot, and missed. As the buzzer rang, my team flooded the floor, and we hugged tight. We'd come back from sixteen points down at the beginning of this quarter, and we'd done it because we believed in ourselves.

Chapter Twenty-Nine

Comeback Kid

For most of my life I've forced myself to be ahead of the game. Even though I'd spent days and weeks clawing back from disappointments like injuries and Lyme disease, those times were greatly outnumbered by the moments when I was light-years ahead of everyone else and everything. Being the Comeback Kid was a foreign feeling. Sure, it was a little bit weird and scary, but for the most part it was exciting.

When you're always on top, or always working to make yourself the star, there's no drama. If you succeed, it's because you were determined not to see any other outcome. Losing or failing isn't an option to you. Unfortunately, that's not just impractical; it's also a recipe for disaster. You're setting yourself up to totally melt down when things fall apart.

During the 2014 play-offs, I loved being the Comeback Kid. The situation was full of possibility. I didn't see it as a source of pressure but rather as a chance to double up on my efforts and prove that I could defy expectations. It was a new identity for me and a way to set a whole new set of goals. And if we lost? Well, that meant we'd have the chance to stage yet another comeback in the future.

That's how I chose to see things after game two of the semifinals. Even though we were riding a high from the previous game's win, we couldn't pull our act together during the second game. We made a strong showing in the first half, but Atlanta went on the attack in the second, led by an amazing player named Angel McCoughtry, who scored a whopping thirty-nine points. In the end we lost fair and square, 93–82, in front of a hometown crowd.

Whether or not we'd advance in the play-offs would be decided by a third game in Atlanta. This matchup would prove to be the biggest comeback of my life, and by the time it was over, fans and the media were calling it one of the best WNBA play-off games of all time.

The fact is, I didn't start the game strong at all, though. The Dream were up 30–17 at the end of the first quarter because they consistently nailed their free throws, which they hadn't in the previous two games. They'd learned from their mistakes, and then they'd capitalized on them.

The second quarter wasn't much better for us. Atlanta's defense got in the way of our attempted rebounds, made ten times more fast breaks than we did, and netted at least two baskets anytime we made one.

The first half bled into the second, and at the end of three quarters, we were still behind by double digits, 67–51.

"We're not done," I said to my team as we huddled up at

the end of the third quarter. "I can see it in all of your eyes. We can come back. But we absolutely have to push—and then finish!"

In the heat of a basketball game, when players are rushing toward the ball or outmaneuvering defenders as they push toward the net, fans often forget about the little things that are necessary to make shots, blocks, and rebounds connect. It's not just the hard work or muscling that moves a game forward—it's also the ability to finish. No ball will go through a basket unless it's aimed just right. No rebound can be made unless you position yourself correctly. Small tweaks and adjustments can make all the difference as you're trying to finish. And that's what I knew we had to do in the last quarter.

Just as we refocused and sprang into action—forcefully but carefully—Atlanta started to stumble. We stopped being afraid to drive into the lane, and Atlanta didn't react fast enough. Soon, with just under seven minutes left in the game, we were down by only ten—a big mental difference from the sixteen we'd trailed by at the end of the third quarter.

Then we unleashed ourselves, scoring twelve unanswered points. The Dream rebounded quickly, and the score bounced back and forth between us as the clock dipped below the one-minute mark. With 29.5 seconds left, the Dream's guard Shoni Schimmel made a beautiful run, jumped, and sunk the shot, bringing their lead to 80–77.

Still, I could sense Atlanta was slipping, very subtly. They'd lost the edge that we still had, and I wanted to capitalize on that. When I got the ball, I drove to the line and made a jumper that brought us to within one point. In order to get the ball back quickly, we fouled one of their point guards, and sure enough, my hunch that they were flagging was right.

The Dream missed both free throws, and we got the ball back with 16.2 seconds left.

After the time-out, Atlanta had a tough choice to make. They could foul me, but since I was eleven for eleven from the free throw line, sending me up for two shots would probably ensure our lead. The other choice was to let us take a chance at shooting and try to stop us with their defense.

When the ball went into play, Courtney Vandersloot took possession and moved to the back of the paint. Looking around for someone to pass to, she saw me on her left, and tossed the ball. When I caught it, I spied Atlanta's Angel McCoughtry in front of me. She was their 6'1" small forward who'd been such a powerhouse scorer in the last game. She blocked me aggressively, and suddenly I thought back to the training I'd had in the off-season.

Go right at her. Be forceful. Don't let her throw you off. You're stronger than you think you are.

I charged ahead, stopped for a brief moment to fake, jumped, and then let the ball leave my fingers. It hung in the air, hit the backboard ever so slightly, and then fell into the basket.

A perfect finish, I thought. *Two points!*

With 8.2 seconds, we'd taken the lead. Unless Atlanta could make a basket on their next possession, the game was ours.

I wonder if they were just tired, or if they were still

scratching their heads from our improbable comeback, but they just couldn't overcome our defense. We swarmed them, and as they shot, I knew there was no way they'd make it. The ball hit the rim, bounced three times, and fell down just as the buzzer rang. My team rushed onto the court, and all I could think was: *We came back! Winning when no one expects you to is simply the best feeling in the world.*

Chapter Thirty

Make Adjustments

If you're a high achiever like me, you probably never want to stop. Everywhere you turn, you likely see a new challenge to tackle, a new skill you want to test out, or a new competition you can't wait to be a part of. As I've said a million times, if you go too fast or push too hard, you might burn out. I've spent the last ten years of my life trying to avoid that; the last thing I want is to quit something midstream just because I've worked way too hard and lost sight of my passion for it. That's why, now, I'm the first person who'll tell you that when you're exhausted, injured, or can't find your way, you need to stop, rest, and reevaluate your situation.

Unfortunately, though, there are times when you need to slow down, but for whatever reason, you just *can't*. You have to learn to adjust instead, and that is exactly what I did during the WNBA play-offs.

During game one of the series against Atlanta, I'd tried to rebound a ball, just like I'd done a few thousand times before in my career. I didn't move differently, wasn't more aggressive than normal, and certainly didn't invite any kind of unwanted physical contact. But at some point while I was jumping up to grab the ball, an opposing player's elbow landed squarely in my back. I winced from the pain, thinking, *Wow, that was sharp!* But I kept on playing, assuming it was just an innocent bump and that I'd feel better almost immediately.

I didn't. My back got tighter and sorer with each passing minute, but it never bothered me so much that I asked to leave the game.

After everything was over, though, I pulled Pokey aside to talk to her.

"My back is hurting after getting elbowed," I said. "I think I need to talk to a trainer about it. It's probably not an issue, but I should get it checked out."

I've had scoliosis for years, meaning my spine is curved a little bit sideways. This throws my posture off, makes my muscles tighten, and causes a slight limp because one leg becomes slightly longer than the other. The fact that I'm so tall and move so much makes having this kind of condition not at all unusual, and I've always just dealt with it by seeing a physical therapist every now and then. But this time the pain felt different. It was stronger and wouldn't go away no matter how much PT I did.

"There's some inflammation," my trainer said after working my sore muscles with her hands. "I think we should try a treatment that's a little more advanced."

She recommended electrostimulation, which involves putting small pads on the site of pain and sending low levels of electricity directly into the muscles. It has a slightly more intense effect than massage, though it still warms and vibrates your sore spots so that they loosen up.

It helped, but not enough. My back was worse than ever when we faced off against the Indiana Fever in what would be one of the most dramatic series in WNBA play-off history.

I was still a little raw about the fact that the Fever had swept us in the play-offs the year before—even though we'd been the better team—so I didn't want to beat them just because it would take us to the WNBA finals. I needed to prove that those three games were just a fluke. I wanted to show the world that we were—then and now—the dominant team.

But the fact that my back hurt so badly made me worry I wouldn't be able to do that.

During game one I scored only fourteen points, and we lost 70–77. I spent what felt like half the game lying on my back on the sidelines, my trainer stretching my muscles, and the other half of the game shuffling—rather than running—around the court. Sylvia Fowles even had to tie my shoes for me before the game because I couldn't bend over.

I decided to have a heart-to-heart with Pokey after the game ended.

"I think you need to play me differently in game two," I told her. "I need to move less, so why don't I become a decoy? I can be stationary, looking like I'm going to catch a pass at any moment, yet no one will ever send the ball to me. I'll just fake everyone out."

She agreed, and the plan worked. The game went into double overtime, and I played thirty-nine minutes of it, yet I scored only nine points. My role was to throw people off, not make baskets, and I did just that. We barely squeaked out a victory, 86–84, ensuring a third game, where the Eastern Conference Championship would be decided.

Having a finals berth on the line is a huge deal, so I knew I couldn't take the time to rest my back. If I could breathe and walk—even slowly—it was crucial that I play.

In times like that, you have to think about your role and strengths differently, then adjust to them. I'd almost always been the leading scorer or the all-around player who kept my team's score high. Or I'd been the Comeback Kid, helping my team rebound from a terrible deficit. During game three I chose to play backup. I'd let other players shine, and I'd support whatever plays they made. Sure, I might suffer through all of it, but I'd buckle down and do my best.

While I gritted my teeth and worked as hard as I could, hoping my back wouldn't start to spasm, I focused on stopping Indiana's top scorer, Tamika Catchings. Then I watched as our point guard, Allie Quigley, outmaneuvered the defense and aggressively drove toward the basket.

This new strategy worked for the team even when I started to falter. During the second quarter, my back hurt so badly I had to sit out through the half and almost all of the third quarter. But it didn't matter. We'd adjusted, and Allie had scored twenty-four points. We'd also pretty much stopped Tamika Catchings, allowing us to clinch a 75–62 victory.

For the first time in its history, the Chicago Sky would be going to the WNBA finals, and I was going to be a part of it.

Chapter Thirty-One

WNBA Finals

The Phoenix Mercury were the winningest single-season team in WNBA history. Their regular season record for 2014 was 29–5, which beat the previous record of twenty-eight wins.

Believe me, they'd earned every single word of praise they got. They worked hard, had great players like Brittney Griner and Diana Taurasi, and they led the league in points per game, overall offense, *and* defense. They'd turned their program around since 2012, when they'd been the second worst team in the WNBA. I didn't feel much other than respect for how good their 2014 season had been, and playing them in the finals was actually going to be an honor.

Everyone expected us to lose. I mean *everyone*—from coaches to other players to almost every sportswriter in the media. We'd had a season plagued with injured players, including me—twice!—and the fact that we were in the finals was practically a miracle. We hadn't led the league in scoring, rebounding, assists, or any of the markers of a championship team, and I was convinced it was pure determination and guts that had gotten us as far as we had. I had no idea if that would carry us through and make us victorious. But I knew I had to shut out all the trash talk I was hearing if I was going to play well.

Having a good attitude before heading into a new or challenging situation doesn't just mean pumping yourself up or telling yourself how amazing you are. It also involves refusing to let the negative chatter of others affect you. Tell yourself: *They don't know me. Only I do.* And then move on and do your best.

I think it's unrealistic to believe you *won't* hear the unpleasant things other people say about you, though. I can't spend the rest of my life refusing to turn on the TV, read the papers, or go online just because I'm worried I'll see something negative about me, my style of play, or my team. After I dropped out of UConn, I tried to hide away, shielding myself from the world, at my parents' house, but that was just silly. By the time I got to the UD campus, people were still talking about me, and I could hear *every* word of it!

But did it make me stop playing or play worse? In the end, no. And that was because I forced myself to shrug it off and do my best.

Before the WNBA finals, we understood that the Mercury were almost perfect. But we knew there was one thing we were better at, and that was rebounds. We knew we could win the five-game series by getting the ball back as quickly and efficiently as we could, then driving to the basket as fast and as skillfully as our legs could carry us.

Unfortunately, that didn't make a difference. Throughout

the three games we played, the Mercury were just so much better than we were.

In game one their field goal percentage was double ours. We actually *did* rebound better than they did, but when you can't get the ball into the basket, being able to rebound doesn't matter. They beat us 62–83, and I was on the bench, nursing a sore back, for all but ten minutes of it.

In game two the Mercury absolutely dominated us. Every single one of their starters, including Brittney Griner and Diana Taurasi, scored in the double digits over the course of the game. Even after Diana Taurasi got into foul trouble early on, and Brittney Griner injured her eye in the first quarter, they still outplayed us. And even when we started to show some momentum in the second half, the Mercury still made basket after basket.

In the end they beat us 68–97.

If there's anything we proved throughout the season—with all of the injuries and setbacks—it's that we were resilient. We'd never give up, no matter what, so we vowed to go into game three fighting.

We thought the path might be clearer because Brittney Griner wouldn't be playing.

"She's had to have retinal surgery," Pokey told us just before game three. "The Mercury just tweeted about it. When she got poked in the eye, it did some real damage."

Even though Brittney's absence was a good thing for us, I still felt a lump in the pit of my stomach. I would never, ever be happy for someone else's misfortune, especially considering all that I'd gone through with my own health. Plus, I was friends with Brittney. We'd sat next to each other during dozens of interviews before and after the WNBA draft—even during a particularly emotional one when she'd come out of the closet. I'd decided to be a little more private about my love life because Amanda wasn't a public figure, but I was happy that Brittney was so open. I wanted her to spread her wings in every part of her life—even on the court against me in the most high-profile game of our lives.

But she wasn't going to get that opportunity, so the Sky would try to capitalize on it.

Without Brittney's amazing blocking, we headed straight for the paint in the first quarter, scoring eighteen out of twenty points close to the net. Sylvia Fowles took charge too, and by late in the first quarter, we were down by only two.

But Diana Taurasi turned on the heat and showed why she was one of the best players in the sport. By the end of the first half, she'd become the all-time leading three-point shooter in the WNBA finals, having scored thirty-eight total.

We were playing better than we had in the first two games; the lead had switched nine times. By halftime we were down by only two points, and a win felt within our reach.

I know we can do this, I thought at halftime. *Even though your back could be better, you can capitalize on the fact that they're not doing as well as they did in the previous games. You're weak, but they're weaker too. Play on that.*

In the third quarter we did. I wonder now if I had a sense that Diana Taurasi was getting tired, but she almost fell apart after halftime, not scoring a single point in the third quarter. She kept handing out turnovers, and after five, I started to wonder if she was actually giving the game to us.

But there was still a lot of time on the clock, so anything could happen.

In the fourth quarter Diana made two beautiful three-point shots and became the WNBA finals scoring leader. We tied the game with thirty seconds left, but it wasn't enough. Another three-point shot from Diana and a pair of successful free throws made the game theirs, and they won 87–82.

Brittney and the other Mercury players on the bench had had their arms wrapped around one another's shoulders in the last breathless seconds, but when the buzzer echoed across the court, they ran to the center of it. As they hugged tight and jumped up and down, I thought about how they must feel.

Winning feels great, I thought, *so while I'm sad that it's not us, they really earned it.*

I didn't just walk off the court and forget about the loss, though. Not winning the finals was a *big* deal, and I really dwelled on it. I knew some problems, like my back, had been out of my control during the series. Other issues had been all my fault. I knew I'd made mistakes, and I could have named every one of them if you'd asked me. But I promised myself I'd get back up and learn from them. I was determined to grow stronger and be the best I could be in 2015.

Thankfully, that would prove to be true in a million different ways.

PART FOUR
SLAM DUNK

Chapter Thirty-Two

Demand Excellence

I've talked so much about burning out that you might assume I spend my life biting my nails, worrying about crashing again. I promise I don't. I've got such strong support and love around me now that balancing and being true to myself can be pretty easy. I handle almost anything a million times better than I did when I was a teenager.

That doesn't mean life is completely stress-free, though. Being an adult is still hard when the going gets tough! Luckily, you can develop skills that will get you through your problems or setbacks. Whatever these practices are—meditation, talking to friends, exercising, even just indulging in a hobby you love—they'll help you stay afloat. Then you can focus on getting to the next level of doing whatever it is you love.

Two years into my life as a professional athlete, that's exactly what I discovered. I needed some new tools under my belt to keep maturing personally and professionally.

After the 2014 season I still didn't want to leave the US, just like in 2013. My decision was mostly because I wanted to go home and see my family, but it was also partly because of a conversation Kobe Bryant and I had recently had on Twitter Messenger.

I'd been watching Kobe play basketball on TV since I was in grade school, and I'd always loved him. He was never afraid of a challenge, and he pushed so hard, with such skill and intelligence, that people either worshipped him on the court or hated his guts. He liked having fans, but he really *loved* having opponents. In fact, he thrived on it. He knew that if people were against him, he must be doing something right, and it just made him play better.

I've always wanted to develop that kind of devil-may-care attitude, but I've never known how to. Maybe it's because I'm shy and introspective, or maybe I'm just hyperaware of how I affect the people around me, but something about being ruthless has always scared me.

One day I decided to find out how by going straight to the source. I tweeted Kobe directly, asking how he dealt with all the haters in his life, and he was nice enough to answer. He was as straightforward and honest as I hoped he'd be, explaining that he knew who he was, so he'd learned not to care what people thought. When I asked what he did to develop that mind-set, his answer was awesome. He told me he'd come up with a power phrase that motivated him. It embodied himself and all that he wanted to do and be, and he always kept it in mind.

I didn't even know what to write back. Elena Delle Donne was a lot of things—a sister, a daughter, a basketball player, a burnout, a comeback kid, a homebody, and a patient—but was there a mantra that pulled all those parts together? Was there one slogan that drove me through every challenge? I couldn't for the life of me think of one.

I knew the answer wouldn't come right away, so I decided to take the summer after the 2014 season—the season that had been the craziest, most up-and-down six months of my entire life—to explore this question. I needed a fresh start and a clear head, and I couldn't get that if I stayed in Chicago. There was no better place for me to be than at home in Delaware.

I wouldn't be sitting on the couch meditating all day, though. I had big plans for the six months before the 2015 season started, and I'd be busy doing things I loved. Just like the year before, I was going to host a sleepover basketball camp for girls at Ursuline, then take a similar camp on the road to five other states. I wouldn't just be teaching basketball skills and coaching practices, though; I also wanted the camps to teach the girls about self-esteem, motivation, and setting realistic goals. I hoped they'd learn from my mistakes and figure out not to push themselves so hard that they lost their passion for the sport.

Given my new position as an ambassador to the Special Olympics, I'd also be expanding these camps to include disabled athletes. Even though there's no way Lizzie would ever be able to shoot or rebound, she'd taught me more than anyone else about the power of the body and mind. I knew that when the girls in my basketball camps saw special-needs athletes reaching their potential—under the most difficult circumstances—they'd be inspired to do their best no matter what.

Finally, I was going to take care of myself. I planned to train every morning with John Noonan, then make regular visits to my physical therapist, ATI Physical Therapy, whose practice I'd gone to for years. I'd lift weights with Dina Saitis, my personal trainer, and of course I'd be no stranger to Rita's office in Pennsylvania. I was *determined* not to let Lyme disease sneak up on me like it had midway through the last season, and I knew that by staying on top of my symptoms with Rita, I could tackle a relapse when it happened.

After all that, my family was going to take a long trip to the Bahamas, and I couldn't *wait* to hit the beach and swim in the ocean.

I had Team Delaware (and Team Pennsylvania!) surrounding me, the love of my mom, dad, Gene, Lizzie, and Amanda, and a goal to be healthy and stronger by the beginning of the 2015 season. I was doing so much in so many different areas, all the while nurturing my spirit. I was happy, rested, and totally open-minded.

Yet for the life of me I couldn't think of any one phrase that motivated me.

What do I want most in life? I asked myself. *What is it that I'm always pushing for?* That question swam around my head all summer.

I knew that I'd gone after so many of the wrong things for way too long. In middle school I'd been searching for a love of basketball that I later realized I'd never find unless I gave it up. When I peeled myself off the bench during the 2014 play-offs, I'd been trying to find the strength and the willpower that would help me overcome my physical limitations. I'd mustered it, but just barely, and then it hadn't really led to much. And during every season on every team I'd ever played with, I'd been shooting for victory. Yet sometimes, like when we'd been swept in the WNBA finals, it was impossible to reach.

Perfection, I suddenly realized. *That's what I've been looking for.*

I knew that a goal like that was totally crazy, though. No one—least of all myself—would ever be perfect. Even Kobe Bryant missed baskets, lost games, and got penalized! He made as many mistakes on the court as I did, yet he still worked his hardest to be the best. Something was driving him, and it wasn't the ability to be 100 percent flawless.

So if my mantra isn't "Seek perfection," what is it? I wondered.

I took my mind off that question for a second and thought about the girls I'd been working with. At each training camp these wonderful kids were so eager and happy to be learning new skills, and they practiced all of them like crazy. Yet working with disabled students was teaching them that success doesn't necessarily stem from the talents you're born with; it comes from trying your hardest—even if you have limitations. All of these girls were amazing, yet none of them had been born perfect, and none of them ever would become perfect. Something still drove them, though. What was it?

Then I remembered a conversation I'd had with Gene after one of our workouts together.

"Gene," I'd said, "Kobe Bryant told me I should find a

power phrase, and I'm totally stumped. I can't figure out why I do what I do."

"Well," he'd answered, "maybe instead of worrying about your intentions, you should just look at your results. Your grades, your relationships, your basketball performance, even how you've dealt with being sick. You're not perfect, but you've done it all—your whole life—with *excellence*."

Suddenly it hit me.

I'm like the kids in my camp; I just want to be excellent. We know we'll never be perfect, but in our individual ways and using very different skill sets, we demand excellence.

I decided that "Demand Excellence" would be my mantra. I was going to do everything in my power to make 2015 the best season I'd ever had, and that wasn't going to come from being flawless. I was human, so I knew I'd make mistakes, but I could keep striving for something that would elevate me to the highest level possible. It wouldn't be perfection, but it could be darn well close to it.

The 2015 season wouldn't just be a little excellent. It would turn out to be the *most* excellent of my life.

Chapter Thirty-Three

You're a Firework

I said my mantra over and over again during the beginning of the 2015 season, and it started to work its magic. While the Sky weren't dominating—we were 3–3 by the time our seventh game rolled around—I was playing the best basketball of my life. For example, I'd been averaging almost thirty points in each game—a career high—and in our second game I'd even netted forty points. I'd also had double-doubles in two games, meaning I made double-digit baskets *and* rebounds. I was demanding excellence from my body and my level of play, and I was seeing results.

At the end of June a home game against the Atlanta Dream would prove that more than ever.

The Sky hadn't secured back-to-back wins all season, and the only thing we wanted was to show the world that we had some momentum. We weren't hoping for a huge streak, and we weren't in a do-or-die situation, but we were starting to feel some desperation. We'd won our last game, though, and we thought that a victory over the Dream would do a lot to lift our spirits.

By the third quarter we were feeling optimistic. We'd been up by as much as seventeen points, but Atlanta was as aggressive as we were. In the last few minutes of the third, they scored sixteen points to our seven, bringing the game to within three. The fourth quarter was back and forth, and when the buzzer rang, we were tied at 86. As overtime began, I realized I needed to push myself into overdrive.

If you're going to demand excellence, now's the time to do it, I told myself.

Overtime in the WNBA is five minutes long, and for the first four minutes, we kept a tight lid on Atlanta and limited them to two points. With 8.6 seconds left, though, they'd almost caught up, and the score was 98–96 when I was fouled and sent to the line.

Now, I'd made seventeen consecutive successful foul shots in this game, which had tied the WNBA record. I'd also scored forty-three points, which was more than I'd made in any other game since college. But every time I'd broken records before, it hadn't happened at the end of a game. Also, my team's pride— or our ability to show that we *could* win two games in a row— had never been on the line. But as I stepped toward the paint, took a deep breath, and grasped the ball before I looked up to shoot, I realized that winning this game might be all up to me.

You've made this shot a million times. Three dribbles. L shape. Lift, and flick. No pressure.

The ball sailed through the air, arced, and went into the basket. I'd put my team up by three *and* broken the single-game free throw record!

I stepped back to the line and raised my arms and the ball. Once again the ball left my fingers, flew through its course, and didn't even hit the rim as, *swoosh,* it went through the basket. Not only had I completed nineteen consecutive free throws, but I'd scored forty-five points in the game, a career high for me and the sixth-highest point total in a WNBA game.

Doing something that monumental didn't feel like taking the world's cutest selfie and posting it to Instagram so everyone could see how great I was. I wasn't looking for tons of praise from total strangers. I'm not playing this sport for the adoration, to break records, or to win prizes. Sure, there's a terrific satisfaction that comes with playing the best you've ever played, but the feeling was more complex than that.

For me, demanding excellence—and seeing results—is about making a positive statement to the public, even when they don't support you.

Players like Kobe and I know that sometimes when you're performing your best, people criticize you the most. They may even insult you, but demanding excellence means you have to put on a brave face and not react. No drama, no lashing out on social media, and no big meltdowns. If you're being bullied or talked about behind your back or online, be brave, hold your head high, and talk to someone—like a teacher, a counselor, your parents—about it. When and if you respond, be balanced. Remaining cool will help you *and* the situation.

After the end of our game against the Dream—the highest

scoring game of my professional career—I learned all of this firsthand.

In the postgame interview, I was asked to read various tweets that tagged the @SportsCenter or @WNBA handles. I'm sure there were hundreds, or maybe thousands, of people who'd tweeted congratulations on my milestone or the Sky's last-second, hard-won victory, but the PR team for the Sky had deliberately pulled together the cruelest, most sexist, and downright stupidest tweets they could find just to show how terrible the Internet can be. They wanted to illustrate how much people want to tear others down when they're doing their best.

Even when I saw the worst tweets, I brushed them off and laughed.

Women aren't capable of playing sports, one tweet said.

Then another: Yeah against what competition. I could score 45 points on them.

The WNBA is a total joke and totally unwatchable.

I think this one was my personal favorite, though: That doesn't look like a kitchen to me.

Even if you're feeling better than you've ever felt, or you're coming off a huge victory, these haters can get you down. There was a small part of me that was sad when I read those tweets. But I don't take them to heart, and you shouldn't either. It's like Katy Perry says: You're a firework, so show 'em what you're worth.

Demanding excellence isn't just about playing well; it

also involves holding your head high before, during, and after your accomplishment, and knowing deep in your heart that—despite what anyone else says—you did your best. Find validation within yourself or through those who support you. Believe me, you deserve the excellence that you demand.

Chapter Thirty-Four

MVP Award

Part of demanding excellence from yourself involves recognizing when you need to improve. After a back-and-forth 5–5 record in June, getting better is exactly what the Sky did. We went 6–3 in July and 7–4 in August—and dropped only two games at home. I wasn't on the scoring tear I'd been on at the start of the season, but I was still incredibly consistent, averaging in the low twenties in almost every game. I hit a few double-doubles both months too, my rebounding continuing to be strong.

By the end of the summer, it was looking likely that the Sky would be going to the WNBA play-offs again. But one thing was looming larger in my mind: the WNBA MVP award, which would be voted on and announced just before the play-offs began. Fans, the media, coaches, and players had been calling 2015 my breakout season, and they'd all put my name at the top of the list for MVP.

The MVP award is the highest honor any professional basketball player can receive during a season. It's voted on by broadcasters and sportswriters who've been watching and studying each player all season. Basketball awards and honors are often a numbers game, so while I haven't asked anyone outright, I'm sure these professionals look to the statistics to narrow down the pool of players. Some things really can't escape their notice, like records being broken, and I'd done that this year. By the end of the regular season in mid-September, I'd missed only eleven foul shots and had a 95 percent success record for free throws, which was the best single-season percentage in WNBA history. In fact, it elevated my career record above Steve Nash's NBA free throw record of 90.43 percent! I really hate bragging, but breaking men's records in a game that people just *assume* men dominate makes me smile.

Winning the MVP award requires more than just facts and figures, though. The voters want a player with leadership and heart, and they look at all-around ability, the team's overall performance, and how that player contributes to the team. If you're a top-notch rebounder but that's really all you can do, you probably won't be MVP. Or if you miss a stretch of games—like I had in 2014—you most likely won't be considered. But players like Sheryl Swoopes, Diana Taurasi, Candace Parker, and Lauren Jackson had all been honored in the past, and they'd distinguished themselves by being dominant and successful everywhere on the court—then leading their team to greatness.

Numbers-wise 2015 had been the best all-around year of my career. Thankfully, it had been my healthiest, too. Lyme disease hadn't sidelined me, and except for some bumps and bruises, I'd been injury-free. Because of this, I'd started in every game, which hadn't happened in the previous two years that I'd been in the WNBA. The Sky hadn't performed as well in 2015 as they had in years past, but they'd improved over the course of the season, and that counted for so much. All told, every statistic, media analysis, and chatter among commentators pointed to the possibility that I'd be honored as the league's MVP.

There's no way, I said to myself when I stopped and really thought about it. *There has to be someone else who deserves this more.* No matter how much my friends, family, and coaches tried to get me to accept that I'd probably win, I just couldn't believe it.

Then, just two days before the play-offs were set to begin, where we'd be facing the Indiana Fever, I got a call.

"Elena," a woman's voice on the other end of the line said, "this is Laurel Richie."

Laurel Richie was the president of the WNBA, a position she'd held for five years. I'd met her many times, but getting a personal call? That was new.

"It's nice to hear from you," I said cautiously. I was pretty certain why she'd rung me up, but I didn't want to assume anything.

"I'd like to congratulate you on being named the 2015 WNBA Most Valuable Player. You deserve it so much, and we're thrilled. I hope you can take the time to celebrate this victory before the play-offs begin."

"Thank you," I answered honestly, even though I was so

shocked that my hands were shaking. "This means so much to me. Really, I'm honored, and I can't believe it."

Almost the second after I hung up, ESPN SportsCenter tweeted the news, and my phone went crazy. I began to get texts, calls, Facebook notifications, and tweets, and I started trending all over the Internet. When I finally had a chance to stop and read some of my messages, I broke out into a huge smile and called Amanda over.

"Hey, Amanda," I said, "look at this. J. J. Watt just congratulated me. Isn't that cool? It's amazing to hear from such an elite athlete from another sport."

I was *so* happy. Like, happier than I'd ever been in my life. I logged on to Twitter immediately and thanked my teammates, naming each of them individually. Then, when the news really sunk in, I looked inward and realized what I wanted to express.

I'm humbled. Winning this makes me understand how insignificant I am compared to the contributions my team made to help me get here. Now I need to return the favor.

For many people a huge prize might make them feel like the king or queen of the world, and they may be content to just sit there, basking in that glow. Sure, I knew my award elevated me to an elite level of athletes, but it also came with responsibility. It was a teaching moment. My team was young, and I had a duty to them. Suddenly I'd been called on to be more of a leader than ever before.

It was a sobering, humbling feeling, especially because we had a huge goal: winning the WNBA Championship.

Chapter Thirty-Five

Radiate Magic

If Chicago's performance in the 2015 play-offs taught me anything, it was that I still had a long way to go before I'd become the kind of leader I wanted to be. I'm not saying I did anything horribly wrong—in fact, I played some great basketball, including scoring a whopping forty points in game three of our three-game series against Indiana. They just displayed a magic we didn't have.

I think much of that talent had to do with their star veteran, Tamika Catchings.

Tamika was a basketball legend, and in 2015, her second-to-last season, she was thirty-six years old. She'd played with Indiana her entire career, including in 2011, when she'd been named the league MVP. Even though she was the oldest person on the court by a long shot, she never slowed down. She was a powerhouse, and members of her team described her work ethic as a warrior mentality.

Maybe there's a certain wisdom that comes with more than a decade of playing professionally, but I don't believe

Tamika's influence is only because of her age. I believe Tamika inspired her team with a razor-edge vision and domination, and her toughness pushed her team to play like they were at war.

And it was a battle they won.

We briefly thought we might have a chance after game one, which we just barely won by five points. But we were tired and beaten down; Tamika had scored twenty-one points, and the Fever's defense had pushed us at every stretch. In game two they beat us by seven, partly because Tamika made twenty-two points and partly because their defense kept me from getting anywhere close to my average shooting record. In game three they bested us, 100–89, and we were officially out of the play-offs. Even though I'd dominated the field with forty points, Tamika and her team's forcefulness had just been too much on the court.

"Catch obviously makes them believe things they never thought they could do, and that's what makes her so special aside from her talent," I told ESPN after the game.

It was true. Her willfulness, her determination, and whatever magic she radiated to her team changed the tide of every game. And after losing in the play-offs long before we'd ever expected, I vowed to try to be more like her the next season.

I want to inspire my team like Tamika does, I thought. *I want to help them—and others—to beat the odds, and to do things they don't think they're capable of. If I've overcome so much in my life, how can I convince a team that they can do the same?*

For the answer to that I had to step off the basketball court.

When I was a kid, my hero was Sheryl Swoopes. Sure, she was an amazing basketball player, but I loved her for the funniest reason, a reason that had nothing to do with how well she played. I worshipped her because she had her own signature sneaker.

"But, Elena," my mom would say, "I thought you liked Sheryl Swoopes because of her scoring records."

"Well, I do," I'd answer, "but I really just want a pair of her Nikes. Air Swoopes are the coolest shoes in the world."

I'm not diminishing Sheryl Swoopes's million accomplishments, or how she changed the game of basketball for girls around the world just like me. But the fact that she'd branded herself and made people notice her—and the new women's league called the WNBA—was so impressive to me.

People don't assume that only men play basketball anymore, I thought every time I laced up my pair of Air Swoopes and headed out the door to practice. *They know now how good female players can be, and that's because of Sheryl.*

Could I capture a little bit of her magic and influence by raising my profile, just like she had?

The timing was definitely right for it. Tamika Catchings was about to wrap up her WNBA career, and Diana Taurasi had taken a year off to play overseas. Viewership of the 2014 WNBA finals had been up 91 percent from three years before, and while it was still more than three hundred thousand viewers short of how many people watched the NBA finals, female basketball was on some fans' radars more than ever.

I'd just been named MVP, and I was already doing a lot. I had endorsement deals, speaking engagements, a basketball academy devoted to training young women, and my work with the Special Olympics and Lyme disease. Every single bit of that helped raise the WNBA's profile, but should I have been doing more?

Absolutely. I knew that the more I started to do off the court, the more it would make people pay attention to what happened on the court. That would make me a highly influential player—just like Tamika—if I played my cards right.

During the off-season I kicked my public profile up a notch.

I interviewed with *Time* magazine, a more serious, higher-profile magazine than I'd met with before. I participated in the Nike Innovation summit, which is an important annual conference that showcases new, groundbreaking advances in athletic gear and technology. I played in the NBA All-Star Celebrity Game with celebrities including Kevin Hart and the Property Brothers from HGTV. Sure, all of this was fun and interesting, but I'd realized that with a larger public profile comes responsibility, and part of that involves helping to drive new fans to the WNBA. Plus, I knew that acting like a star player would inspire everyone, from my young teammates to the little girls who asked me for autographs after games.

The six months before the 2016 season were so different from the year before, when I'd holed myself up in Delaware to get my body strong for the next season. Tamika Catchings's magic had worn off on me, and I realized I was ready for a new role. I wanted to be a truly influential leader—and then I wanted to take home a WNBA Championship trophy.

But first I had to go to the biggest, most magical, most prominent event in the world: the Summer Olympics.

Chapter Thirty-Six

Be Yourself

I was six years old when the 1996 Olympics came to Atlanta, and that summer I spent two full weeks glued to the TV in my family's living room. Sure, Sheryl Swoopes, Lisa Leslie, and Rebecca Lobo—who were on the US women's basketball team—were my idols, and I was thrilled when they beat Brazil in the gold medal game. But it wasn't basketball that stole my heart. Instead I was totally, completely infatuated with the Magnificent Seven—the US women's gymnastics team.

The US gymnastics team had never won an all-around gold medal, and when Shannon Miller, Kerri Strug, Dominique Dawes, and the rest of their teammates headed into the all-around competition, I was breathless. As they entered the final rotation—the vault—I thought I was going to have a heart attack when Kerri Strug injured her ankle on her first attempt. When she stuck the landing on her second flawless try, then collapsed to the ground in pain, I broke out in tears.

"Mom," I cried, "that was the greatest moment of my life.

Kerri Strug just won the gold medal for the US. She's my hero! I want to be a gymnast too."

I was probably too emotional, staring at the TV while Bela Karolyi carried Kerri Strug in his arms to the medal podium, to notice my mom's reaction. I'm sure she started laughing, and I know she told that story to all of her friends and family for the next year. I mean, Kerri Strug was 4'8". At age six I think I was already taller than her! But she *inspired* me, and the idea of going to the Olympics became a two-decade dream of mine.

On April 27 I'd find out whether or not it would become true.

The US women's basketball team had won forty-one consecutive Olympic games and racked up a total of five gold medals, so there was no question that they were the perpetual team to beat. In the 2016 Olympics, which would be held in Rio de Janeiro, the team would be coached by Geno Auriemma, my college coach of all of twenty-four hours. I was one of twenty-five finalists for the twelve-woman squad, and the media kept questioning whether or not it would be awkward if I was on a team with Geno.

"We've always had a great relationship. He's always been respectful of my decision," I said honestly when interviewed by Julie Foudy, a former Olympic soccer star, at an ESPN event. I knew people just wanted a good, juicy story, but they weren't going to get that. Geno had looked past everything that had happened. He knew I'd just been a confused, burned-out kid back then.

Still, Foudy questioned whether that was really true.

"Maybe our first hug was a butt-out hug," I joked in response. "But I figured it out from there."

Like I said before, if the world demands drama, just be a firework and rise above it.

What I couldn't shake off was that being on a new team involved a learning curve, and that was a little intimidating. It *always* was, though; I'd felt a tinge of nervousness every time before the WNBA All-Star Game. I didn't know who I was supposed to be, and I never felt like I was familiar enough with my teammates. I like being aware of everyone's tendencies and knowing where each player needs to be in order to be successful. It was also tough to determine how vocal I needed to be, while still respecting everyone's boundaries and personal preferences.

In the training camp just before the final team cut was announced, those growing pains were more apparent than ever.

"Stop passing the ball so much," Tamika Catchings said to me at one practice. "We want you to do what you do best."

She was right. I knew I had to stomach the fact that I was still figuring out how I fit in on this team and how to be myself on the court. I shrugged off my modesty and played like no one was watching, and sure enough, on April 27, I was named to the US women's national team, along with Tamika, Diana Taurasi, Sylvia Fowles, Brittney Griner, and seven other women.

My dream has come true, I thought. Then I laughed to myself. *Too bad it's not for gymnastics!*

The Olympics were going to be held right smack in the middle of the WNBA season, but the league had made accommodations for that. There would be a five-week break so that the national team could practice, play a few exhibition games (including one at UD!), travel to Brazil, and compete in the Olympics. I knew I'd be busy, but I was thrilled. I wasn't doing any of it out of a sense of duty. I *wanted* this, so it would be a joy.

Unfortunately, that entire summer the Sky didn't perform well, and a little voice inside me began to worry that I was at fault. We were 2–5 at the end of May and 11–13 at the end of July. We hadn't had a losing record the entire time I'd been with the team, yet here we were, struggling in more than half of our games. I started to wonder, was my excitement about the Olympics distracting me, hurting my play, or taking me away from Chicago emotionally?

You can't think that way, Elena, I finally told myself. *It's like Tamika said. Basketball is a team sport, and as long as you're being true to yourself as a player, you're doing your part for the team.*

I was doing *more* than just my part, though. I'd actually been the scoring and rebound leader in many of our games, and injuries hadn't sidelined me at all. It had to be something else. At first Pokey blamed it on our defense. Then as that started to improve, our frontcourt struggled. She finally placed a rookie named Imani Boyette in the center position, and she helped us stay afloat during games.

A winning streak will have to wait, I decided.

As I headed into the Olympics that August, I vowed not to lose sight of the Sky. I was determined to balance the demands of both teams, then win gold on one and make it to the playoffs on the other.

The first goal seemed totally possible; the second would be more challenging and just a little bit tricky.

But before I tackled either, my personal life—once again—would be taking center stage.

Chapter Thirty-Seven

Engagement

Early on in high school, I realized that I really *was* attracted to girls—that it wasn't just some feeling that would pass in a week or so—but I didn't tell my family or any of my friends. I've never been good at confrontation or coming clean about something that's weighing on me, so I've always just not talked about whatever issue is at hand. I convince myself that if I pretend something's not happening, no one will notice.

That's why I waited till after college, when I'd met Amanda and was sure we'd spend our lives together, to come out to my parents. I never wanted to hide her or our relationship, so I hoped that introducing her—and being truthful about who I am—wouldn't be weird.

It wasn't. I think my parents had always suspected it, and Dad didn't seem shocked at all. Mom was initially nervous that I'd be judged by other people—especially all the haters on the Internet who loved to mock me—but then she saw how happy I was. She knew that with Amanda I'd always be able to handle any negativity that would come my way.

After raising one disabled daughter and one daughter

who's a head taller than most men, Mom knew exactly what to say. She was just as supportive as she's always been about me being different.

"In this family," she said, "we celebrate uniqueness. We're all different in one way or another, and we love and honor each other because of that."

When Amanda and I got together, I didn't make a big deal publicly about it. She wasn't a public figure like me, so I didn't want to make a show of her or all that we'd built together. (Like our two dogs, our apartments in Chicago and Delaware, and the fact that she'd become the director of the Elena Delle Donne Academy!) If our relationship was going to be out in the open, we decided it would happen organically, slowly, and naturally. Sure, I'd put a few photos of us hanging out, doing fun things, on Instagram, but that was just because we were always together. It would have been weird not to include her!

So when *Vogue* interviewed me for a profile piece a month or so before the Olympics, we decided there was no way to dodge the fact that we'd gotten engaged early that summer. Yep, that's right; I'd proposed to Amanda, and she'd done the same to me.

In June, Amanda had asked me to go with her to the Montrose Dog Beach. It was still one of our favorite spots, and we walked Wrigley and Rasta there all the time. As we made our way toward a quiet spot away from the hordes of people who sit by the lake in the early summer, Amanda turned to me with a big smile on her face.

"Hey, look at Wrigley," she said.

"Huh?" I was confused. When he stood on his hind legs, Wrigley was as big as me. There was no way to avoid his huge body, so I was basically *always* looking at him.

"His collar," Amanda laughed.

I stared down as Wrigley looked up, and I saw the most beautiful diamond ring I've ever seen hanging from his neck. Before Amanda even had a chance to open her mouth, I screamed.

"Yes! Yes, I'll marry you!"

A few weeks later I decided that Amanda deserved to be as surprised as I'd been, so I decorated our condo's roof deck and assembled a huge dinner of all our favorite foods, including crab legs, Portillo's cheese fries, and doughnuts from a tiny bakery called the Doughnut Vault. Then I invited her up. When we'd finished off every delicious bite, I went back downstairs and came up again with Rasta, whom I'd dressed up in a white veil and train. I held up a sign that read MARRY ME? and presented her with *her* engagement ring.

Then I took a photo of Amanda and Rasta, who hated her costume from the first second I put her in it, and posted it on Instagram.

You know what's so funny? I got lots of likes and congratulations, yet the media didn't pick the story up. No tabloid or news source even acknowledged our engagement till we met with *Vogue*.

That's exactly how I wanted it, I thought. *Just be natural about this, and no one will make a fuss.*

I've worked hard my whole life to achieve balance, not to

break down or burn out again, and to keep my life as steady and sane as possible, and I think a good relationship has gone a long way toward making that happen. Amanda keeps me grounded, makes me laugh, and is a partner in everything I do. You may get frustrated looking for love, but I think it's important to always strive for it. You *will* find it! Your special person doesn't have to be a boyfriend or girlfriend, though; he or she could be a friend, family member, or even a community group. You can create any kind of network you want! Just remember that good people around you can stabilize you.

And as I headed into the Olympics—the biggest athletic event of my entire life—Amanda was my rock.

Chapter Thirty-Eight

Rio

Even though the 2016 Summer Olympics were being held in one of the most beautiful cities in the world, there was a huge shadow hanging over the games: the outbreak of Zika. Brazil was devastated when it was revealed that many women infected with this mosquito-borne illness had given birth to babies with severe birth defects. The Brazilian government did everything it could to contain it—and scientists assured the world that unless you were pregnant, your only risk was the possibility of developing flu-like symptoms—but a lot of people still worried.

After battling a horrible, life-changing illness—carried by an insect, no less—I definitely had second thoughts about going. *I can't get sick again*, I thought. *What if I catch Zika and it interacts with one of the Lyme disease–related illnesses I already have? What if the combination makes me even sicker?*

I talked to Rita about it, and she was reassuring.

"There's been a tremendous amount of research done on Zika," she said. "So far I haven't seen anything to suggest that it will make your illnesses worse."

Informed, I decided to go to Rio. I realized that in almost any situation, there are hundreds, if not thousands, of little issues you can make yourself crazy about, but taking them all seriously is a recipe for a complete meltdown. So I decided to focus on one thing: following the Olympic dream I'd had since I was a kid.

The entire USA basketball program—men's players, women's players, officials, support staff, coaches, and families—would be staying on a 160-person cruise ship that would be docked near the Olympic Village. How could I even think about missing that? The ship had been a tradition since 1992, but the aura around it grew every year. It had restaurants, a swimming pool, several decks, and workout space right there for whenever you needed it. My teammate Sue Bird called it a "bo-tel," which we all thought was hilarious. Being on it would be a vacation, even though I'd be working harder than I ever had in my life.

The way the basketball competition worked at the Olympics was a little confusing, so bear with me while I explain it. In the opening stage, called the group stage, there were twelve teams separated into two groups. Each team would play every other team within its group once. For each matchup, the team that won would get two points, and the team that lost would get one point. The four teams with the most points in each group would then advance to the knockout stage, which consisted of quarterfinals, semifinals, and then the gold medal match.

Like I said before, the US was considered by almost every

major news organization to be the likely winner. We didn't have just history on our side; we had twelve women who played professionally year-round (or in my case, half the year) at the top of the sport. We had the best coach in the world in Geno, and because ten of the twelve women on the team played overseas in the off-season, they understood how international officiating worked. Several of my teammates were also Olympic veterans, so they didn't have the first-time jitters that I had. They knew what they were getting into, and they were prepared.

We had the edge, and we showed it right away in the group stage. First we defeated Senegal with a score of 121–56, which was the biggest margin of victory ever recorded in the Olympics. During that game I slipped up a little when I leaned into a screen, which in the US wouldn't be considered an offensive foul. But in the Olympics it was, and I got penalized. Still, it was my first Olympic game, and I learned something. That was what mattered.

Then we defeated Spain, by forty points, and followed up with victories over Serbia, Canada, and China. We passed right into the knockout round having never trailed after the first quarter of any game.

The quarterfinals weren't difficult either. We breezed right past Japan, 110–64, then met 2012's silver medalists, France, in the semifinals. They put up a strong fight, though, and at halftime we were up by only four. We drilled down on their defense in the third and fourth quarters, then poured on the points and beat them 86–67. Diana Taurasi broke an overall Olympic scoring record too when she made her twenty-eighth point off a three-point shot. The record had stood at twenty-seven for the whole Olympics—and Diana still had the chance to take it even higher, since we had one game left to play!

The US was due to meet Spain in the gold medal game on August 20, and we all suspected we'd beat them, since we'd been so dominant against them in the group stage. My nerves were on fire, though. This was the *Olympics*, Amanda and my whole family (except for Lizzie) were in the stands, and I was playing for my country, not just my school or a city I'd only called home for a few years. Little girls were watching and dreaming the same big dreams I'd had twenty years before, and when we won—*if* we won—I suspected they'd feel the same shivers I would when the national anthem began playing during the medal ceremony.

I knew there was one thing that could take the heat off a big moment like this. I had to develop a completely different mind-set from what I'd had in any other game. In fact, I'd need to get comfortable with the idea of myself as a benchwarmer— not that that was a bad thing! Most of the players on the US team were veterans, with more experience than me, and I was the new kid, not expected to be the star. No one thought I'd play the bulk of the game like I had usually done. I'd come off the bench when I was needed, play my heart out, then step back, rest, and let someone else shine. It wasn't unlike my place in my family or in my relationship with Amanda; my role was just one part of a bigger puzzle.

Honestly, it felt good to be a support player. It wasn't that I knew the pressure was off me. I'm used to stress. I've learned how to deal with it. Sometimes I even like it! It's just that watching other people lead a team to victory is so exciting. When you're on the bench, you can step back and enjoy the game like a spectator would, but at the same time you can learn the moves, the tricks, and the strategies of players you've typically only been up against or playing with. You can really spend time figuring out where you fit in.

It's the same mind-set I talk about with the kids in my clinics.

"When you're on the bench, don't feel like it's because you're not good enough," I say. "Being on the sidelines is actually an opportunity for you to watch and learn how to improve your level of play."

Still, I got so excited when I was called off the bench in the earlier matchups, and I'd started to do things I didn't normally do in games. I set more screens. I played more defense. Then I sat back and watched veterans like Diana Taurasi, Sue Bird, and Tamika Catchings become the score, assist, and rebound leaders.

You know what? It was fun 99 percent of the time! And when it was challenging, I was always learning something, just like all the other Olympic rookies.

"We're still young. We're still learning. We just got our diapers off," Brittney Griner joked in an interview, and even though I laughed when I heard that, I agreed.

But we wouldn't feel like babies in the gold medal game against Spain. We'd feel like part of the greatest women's basketball team in the world, which is exactly what we proved we were.

Chapter Thirty-Nine

Gold Medal Game

The gold medal game against Spain wasn't half as easy as our previous matchups had been.

For the first thirteen minutes, the game was incredibly close, and as I sat on the bench and watched the score tie up six times, then the lead change four times, I got a little worried. The second quarter changed that. Led by Diana Taurasi's and Lindsay Whalen's beautiful shooting, as well as Spain's repeated turnovers, we started to pull away. Spain crept up within three points in the second quarter, but by halftime we were up 49–32. But to all of us, it just wasn't enough.

At halftime our assistant coach approached me.

"Elena," he said, "get in there and play great pick-and-roll defense. Rebound as much as you can. Be aggressive. We need you to help us pour on the points in the second half."

Sometimes coaches have a way of pinpointing exactly what it is that will inspire a player, and when he said that, I felt so motivated. Throughout the Olympics I'd been a role player, helping to support my team, but he clearly saw exactly how I could help us seal our victory and walk to the gold medal podium.

He knows how fired up I am, I thought. *He understands I can be as dominant as every other player out there.*

I practically leaped off the bench, and when I took to the floor, I could feel everyone's momentum shift. Suddenly we were making basket after basket. I netted six points and swatted away a shot from one of the tallest players on the Spanish team. Diana Taurasi hit two more three-pointers, and we went fourteen for eighteen from the field. Not just that; we held Spain to 33.3 percent shooting, and by the end of the third, we'd extended our lead to 88–57.

Even though Spain outscored us 23–20 in the fourth quarter, it just wasn't enough to make up for the damage we'd done in the third. When the final buzzer rang, we had won solidly by a score of 101–72.

I can't believe it, I thought. *This is one of the greatest feelings of my life.*

I wasn't the only person who felt that way. When Tina Turner's "(Simply) The Best" started blasting through the arena, Brittney Griner ran up to me, pulled me close, and lifted me into the air. I didn't know it at the time, but at that moment someone photographed us and posted it online. That image became one of the most iconic moments of the gold medal game *and* the Olympics.

When we walked to the podium to receive our gold medals, I was practically shaking from head to foot. I looked up into the stands and could see my mom and dad, with Gene and Amanda and my sister-in-law and aunt beside them, and I remember tears coming into my eyes as I stepped up.

When my name was called, I leaned down and felt a gold medal placed around my neck. I lifted it up gently, turning it in my fingers and watching it shimmer in the lights that were streaming down from up above.

This doesn't feel real, I thought. *It's like I'm dreaming.*

But when "The Star-Spangled Banner" began to ring through the stadium and I saw the American flag rise, I knew I was an Olympic champion.

Chapter Forty

In an Instant

If you've ever accomplished a huge goal, you might worry that going back to real life will be a letdown. You've just reached the top of the world, so doesn't that mean that everything will be downhill from there?

I could have felt this way after the Olympics. After all, I'd been having the time of my life for two straight weeks, living it up on a cruise ship, playing with the world's top basketball players, and then winning a huge game in front of 10.2 million TV viewers. That was twenty times the number of people who'd watched the WNBA finals the year before!

Then suddenly I had to go home, rest for all of one day, and go back to my day job. Was I disappointed? Not for a second. That was because I'd decided not to view my life after the Olympics as something less exciting than where I'd just been, but instead as a step into something greater. I knew that I'd learned skills at the Olympics that would help me be a better leader for the Sky, and I understood that those skills would make me continue to grow for the next four years. And maybe after that—in 2020—I'd get another shot at going to the Olympics. Besides, I had a pretty daunting opportunity ahead of me, and it was going to take all of my newfound knowledge.

I had to help get Chicago into the play-offs.

Remember that we'd been having a rocky—and losing— season so far. The top four teams in the Eastern Conference would be advancing to the play-offs, and we knew that if we had any shot whatsoever, we needed to have a winning season. We had eleven games left to play, and every single one of them mattered. If we didn't turn our season around, we'd be going straight into the off-season.

I'm not sure if it was the five weeks of rest my teammates had taken while they'd been on break, the skills I'd developed at the Olympics, or just a general fire in our bellies, but we got back onto the court looking great and won our remaining two games in August. After that we won two more! Suddenly our record was 15–13, and the play-offs started to feel like a real possibility.

But if there's anything I know from all the ups and downs I've experienced throughout my career, it's that your situation can change in an instant.

On September 7 we were playing against the Washington Mystics, a team whose chance of going to the play-offs was slimmer than ours. But they were putting up a fight, and eight minutes into the game, I dove onto the ground for a loose ball, and my thumb jammed into the floor. Pain shot through my hand. I couldn't reach for the ball, much less gain control of it, and I knew right away something was wrong.

When the ball went out of bounds, I walked to the sidelines, hanging my head and clutching my hand.

"Pokey, I can't play. Something's really wrong with my thumb."

Pokey and I had developed such a strong relationship that she knew just by looking at me if I was sick. If I came to practice with a glassy look in my eyes, she understood right away that Lyme disease was about to attack. She took my health seriously, and that meant she took *me* seriously.

"Okay," she said, "let's get a trainer to look at it."

While I was being checked out, I missed the rest of the game, and the Mystics tramped all over us, 118–81.

"You tore the UCL, a ligament in your thumb," a doctor said later. "You're going to be day-to-day." Sure enough, I missed the next game too, and we lost 95–88.

Getting into the play-offs is a matter of skill, but also luck. As luck would have it, other teams in our conference—who'd had similar records to ours—had started to slip in the rankings. When they did, our chances of making it into the postseason went up. After we won our next game, we got the best news in the world: we'd sealed our bid for the play-offs.

But whether or not *I'd* be there was still a question.

Chapter Forty-One

Bad Things Will Happen

Because the Sky had climbed our way back to a winning season by the skin of our teeth, we'd managed to end up with the number-four ranking in the league. That meant we advanced automatically into the second round, skipping the single-game elimination that existed in the first round. In the second, more advanced round we'd compete in a single-game elimination against one of our biggest competitors, the Atlanta Dream.

Earlier in the season, in June, we'd had a thrilling last-second overtime victory against the Dream. And we hadn't just won that game against them. We'd beaten them again, 90–82, in our first matchup after the Olympics. Defeating them twice, though, didn't mean we were necessarily the better team. In fact, we'd lost an early-season game against them, and if you added up the total points of all four games, they'd *outscored* us! They were aggressive on offense, and they had the highest average points per game against us in the entire league. We knew the key to victory would be to outmaneuver them on offense *and* defense. We couldn't let them make baskets, and we'd have to double up our efforts to get as many points on the board as possible.

I was dying to play. Even though most of the season had been rocky, we had so much momentum coming off the end of the season. *This* could be our year to win the finals. I just knew it.

Unfortunately, I wouldn't get the chance to be a part of that. I'd been told by one doctor that I should wear a splint on my hand for four to six weeks—which would bench me for the rest of the season—so I'd sought a second opinion from a specialist. That doctor had recommended a surgery that would fix the tear for good *and* might let me play in the championships—if we got there. I needed that sliver of hope that I might be back by the finals, so I chose surgery. It was a tough decision that I agonized over, but I knew what was the best decision for my body, so I trusted myself.

I think you have to realize that just when you're sure that things can't get worse, they might. I'm not saying you should be on your toes at all times, expecting awful things, but just be aware that setbacks happen. Then be prepared for them as much as you can. If you don't, the next disappointment might absolutely destroy you.

I was calm and collected before my surgery. I knew having an operation and being sidelined for a few play-off games weren't the worst things that could happen to me, and I didn't let them throw me off. That's why when something *else* bad came up, I didn't crash. I dealt with it.

This new setback was something I never in a million

years would have seen coming: my private medical details were leaked by a group of Russian hackers. You read that correctly. Right around the time of my surgery, a group of Russian hackers broke into the Olympic drug testing database and released the confidential records of a number of high-profile Olympians, including Simone Biles, Venus and Serena Williams, and little old me. Then the hackers published the name of a drug I take for one of my Lyme disease–related conditions—something that had been banned in competition except in special cases like mine—and the World Anti-Doping Agency had to investigate.

Officials were quick to answer.

"[We] can confirm . . . that the athletes mentioned did not violate any anti-doping rules during the Olympic Games Rio 2016," said the International Olympic Committee in a statement.

Of course I hadn't broken the rules. I'd had what was called a "therapeutic use exemption," and I'd been following doctor's orders. But someone out there had been trying to tarnish the reputation I'd worked so hard to maintain, and that hurt. On top of that, I'm a very private person, and it made me crazy that my life could be and had been broken into—literally.

Between that and missing the beginning of the play-offs, I could have fallen apart. But I didn't. I was prepared, balanced, and knew that, like all bad things, this too would pass.

The would-be scandal not only went away, but life also

got better. I sat on the sidelines and watched the Sky beat the Dream in a thrilling, hard-won 108–98 victory. Chicago would be moving on to the semifinals against the Los Angeles Sparks, and if we won that, we'd advance to the WNBA finals.

Chapter Forty-Two

Shake-Up

We didn't win the semifinals. We lost game one by twenty points, were defeated 84–99 in game two, and then shocked everyone by winning game three in a four-point-margin stunner. But Los Angeles had two WNBA MVPs in Candace Parker and Nneka Ogwumike, had had an unbelievable 26–8 season (compare that to our 18–16 season!), and hadn't reached the finals since 2003, so they were *really* eager. They crushed us in game four, 95–75, and I can't say I was all that surprised.

I think they just wanted it more than we did, I thought. *I think they were prepared to fight harder.*

I stewed for days about losing the series. I kicked myself that I hadn't been able to play, and I wondered what—if anything—I could have done to prevent us from losing. I *hated* not being in control. Then I realized I was being too hard on myself—and my team. We'd worked like crazy to save ourselves from a losing season. We'd turned things around when no one had expected us to, and we'd persisted through injuries and illnesses, with our rookie players rising to the occasion time and time again. We had even taken a team that had gone 11–0 in the beginning of the season to a major showdown in the semifinals. Everyone had assumed that LA was unbeatable, but we proved otherwise! We had a lot to be proud of, and even though we hadn't reached our goal of winning the WNBA championship, we *were* winners.

Be happy with that, I told myself. And I was.

I'd need to keep that attitude more than ever during a series of staff changes in the Sky organization just after the end of our season.

As you know, I'd worked closely with the Sky's assistant coach Christie Sides over the course of my time in Chicago. She'd become my training partner before the 2014 season and had pushed me toward a more aggressive, in-your-face style of play than I'd used in the past. I owed a big part of my 2015 MVP season to her.

Two days after the season ended, my teammates and I found out that Christie was leaving the Sky. She'd been offered a job as the assistant women's coach at Northwestern, and she'd taken it.

In professional sports, loyalty is a tricky thing. People expect you to abide by the terms of your contract and not break it, but taking a new job when your contract ends is both understandable and totally acceptable. Christie had thrived during her time with the Sky, but Northwestern was offering a package she couldn't refuse. She had to accept it. Her move wasn't selfish and didn't break any kind of trust. It was logical, even smart. I was happy for her. She deserved a great job, and Northwestern was offering that.

In late October, though, even bigger news broke—and it sent ripples through our team and the whole WNBA.

Pokey Chatman had been fired. After six seasons with the Chicago Sky, her contract was terminated, and she was forced to look for a new job.

It's not unusual to fire a head coach. If you have losing season after losing season, huge player turnover, or cause infighting or general disruption within your team, your contract might be broken or just not extended. But Pokey had turned a perpetually losing team around. She'd led the Sky to their first play-off appearance in 2013 and their first finals in 2014. In 2015, Sylvia Fowles had shocked our team by sitting out half the season so that she could be traded, and Pokey had dealt with that with grace. And the 2016 season had been a big mess of injuries and ups and downs, but she'd handled it—then led us to a winning season.

Now she was leaving, and the media was fishing for answers.

"Is it because Elena Delle Donne is unhappy with her?" some media speculated.

That wasn't it. I respected Pokey as a coach. Plus, whatever the speculation, no single player has that kind of power. At the Chicago Sky a firing was the decision of the team's owner.

"It was because she never brought home a championship trophy," other media declared.

I realized that must have been it. When you turn a team

around and start winning, owners expect you to take the franchise all the way. They want a championship, and they won't settle for anything less than that.

In the WNBA—as with most professional sports teams—expectations are sky-high. If you want to be an elite coach or athlete, you have to prove that you can lead a team to victory after victory, then win the biggest prize of all. Pokey understood this, so she was more than gracious when she got the news.

"I'm good," she said in one interview. "I can hold my head high. I am proud of our players and what we were able to accomplish. But at the end of the day, we weren't able to get a championship."

The Sky's owner, Michael Alter, thanked her repeatedly—publicly and privately—but he acknowledged what everyone had suspected: that he felt Pokey couldn't take them to a championship. He wanted more, and he thought the team needed a shake-up for that to happen.

Maybe these things are destined or just part of the system, but honestly, it was hard. We knew there would be another head coach, as there always was, but change and saying goodbye are always stressful. That's why I'm glad everyone handled it so rationally, never fueling the rumor mill, lying, or trying to destroy anyone's reputation. Not making tons of drama out of something that just *happens* can make the transition even smoother.

I'd need to remember that as I began to wonder whether it would be time for me to say good-bye to Chicago too.

Chapter Forty-Three

Take a Risk

Sports contracts are complicated, and I don't want to bore you *too* much, but I need to describe them just a little bit so you'll understand what I was dealing with just after Pokey got fired.

When I was drafted by the Chicago Sky in 2013, I signed a contract that bound me to them for four seasons. If I left the team anytime within those four years, I could be penalized in all kinds of ways. I'd had no desire to go, of course, so that wasn't an issue. But when the 2016 season ended, I became what they call a "restricted free agent," which meant that I could be traded to any other team within the WNBA. If Chicago matched that team's offer, I would have to stay with them. If they didn't, I could leave.

There was one other option, though. I could choose to sit out the 2017 season if I didn't get a deal I wanted. Then, when the off-season began, I would become a free agent, and any of the eleven other WNBA teams could vie for me. Other players, like Sylvia Fowles, had done this in the past, and it was really the only way for a restricted free agent to control her destiny.

Some people call sitting out selfish, and in some ways it is. But it's also a big decision and a strategic move. I knew if I sat out, I wouldn't get paid by my team or by the companies I had endorsements with; I also couldn't bear the thought of letting my teammates down.

I really hoped I wouldn't have to make that choice. I'd loved living in Chicago. I had a home there, I'd met my future wife there, and I'd even named my dog after one of its most famous landmarks. I'd built a career with a team that had embraced me with open arms from moment one, and its coaches, owner, and players had helped me reach almost all of my goals—from becoming MVP to going to the Olympics. I owed them so much, and almost every day I pinched myself for how lucky I'd been for four straight years.

But my rookie contract had ended, and it was like the universe had suddenly presented a new, uncharted course to me. I could explore it if I wanted to.

Did I, though? I wasn't sure.

I've done so many interesting things in my life, but I've never considered myself a huge risk taker. I'd so much rather be sitting at home watching old movies with my family than jumping out of airplanes or taking crazy last-minute vacations. My decisions have always been careful and considered, and, most of all, driven by my gut.

I wasn't sure *what* my gut was saying about Chicago, though. If I stayed there, I'd be happy, but was something else calling me?

Opening my options up to teams other than Chicago was

a risk too. I might not get a terrific offer from a team where I wanted to be, and Chicago might not counteroffer. Or I could receive an offer from somewhere I knew I'd love, but Chicago would match, meaning I'd have to choose to take Chicago's offer or sit out. Finally, it was almost unheard of for a top WNBA player—let alone one who'd become MVP, like me—to leave a team after just a few years. For no reason in particular, WNBA culture had dictated that players sign contracts with one team and stay put for most, if not all, of their careers. No elite player had ever switched teams before age thirty-six, when they were in the twilight of their careers, and even then only two women had done it. You were just expected to stay with one team forever. Would a move be viewed as a betrayal, even though there were no concrete rules barring me from doing it?

There were so many possible scenarios that my head was spinning. I started to feel like I had before the WNBA draft, when I'd suddenly realized that, for the first time in my life, I wasn't fully in control of my future. All the opportunities before me were risky, controversial, or just plain scary.

And I still have no idea what I want to do, I thought.

People who like to be in control, like me, have a hard time when the future isn't totally clear. But I've grown to realize that sometimes conclusions just make themselves evident when the time is right. A door may open when you least expect it, or a relationship or situation might suddenly shift, revealing your answer. But you can't force it. You just have to sit back and wait for it to happen.

In early December the Sky announced their new head coach. Her name was Amber Stocks, and she was a former player from the University of Cincinnati who'd been an assistant coach for the Los Angeles Sparks for the previous two years. Apparently she'd been a long-shot choice when Michael Alter had begun interviewing because her résumé was much thinner than other candidates', but she'd won him over. They saw eye to eye and agreed about what Chicago needed. One of those needs was a stronger defense. The other was what she called "a championship culture," meaning building a team that would, no question, remain in the top of the league year after year. To do that, they'd need players who were heavily invested in the franchise and who, above all, really *wanted* to be there.

They're looking for players who are truly passionate about this team, I realized. *Yet there's a little voice in my head saying that that's not me.*

Why? Because, once again, I missed home. I longed for Lizzie, Mom and Dad, and Gene. I wanted to be near my clinics, my doctor, my trainer, and everyone who had nurtured me since I was a little girl. But most of all, I wanted to get married and start another chapter of my life close to my favorite place in the world: Delaware.

Suddenly, just by acknowledging that I had second thoughts about Chicago, I knew I wasn't fully committed. It reminded me of my one day at UConn, when the Huskies captain had told us to play with passion, and I'd realized I had none of it. I just *couldn't* be that wishy-washy player again. I had to open myself up to other options, or I'd become miserable, and then I'd burn out—big-time—for the second time in my life.

In mid-December, just three days after the Sky welcomed Amber Stocks, I made a decision. I was going to shock the basketball world by announcing that I was prepared to leave Chicago.

Just go for it, Elena, I thought. *You shook up basketball eight years ago when you left UConn. Why not do that again?*

So I did.

Chapter Forty-Four

The Mystics

I didn't commit to leaving Chicago immediately. Though my mind was pretty much made up, I needed to be vague to keep my options open, so I spoke carefully.

"Some things will be moving forward for me," I said on a radio show. "I've loved playing with my teammates. There's a great group of young women there. And hopefully with Amber and a new system, it'll be great for them. But for me, wherever I end up, I'll be ready to play basketball."

In my lifelong quest for balance, I've always tried as hard as possible to be gracious. Sure, I knew that my announcement that I was prepared to leave the Sky would cause drama, but I didn't want the *way* I said it to be harsh or sudden. I needed to be measured and thankful, not provocative. After all, if I sounded cool, that's how I'd surely feel. Right?

The truth was that I did. I even felt relaxed, and I decided to leave town for Christmas. Amanda and I went to Disney World and spent a fantastic few days riding rides, stuffing our faces, and wandering through the parks, feeling a million miles away from whatever was going to happen in my future.

When we left Florida, we flew to my parents' place, where we enjoyed a massive Christmas feast with my family. We spent days lounging in front of the fire, pulling together details for our wedding, and dreaming of a new life in 2017.

"Whatever happens," Amanda said, "we'll do it together. We're here for each other no matter what."

I'd made it clear throughout my career how important home was to me. I didn't do it only by going back to Delaware every off-season, or by keeping an apartment near my parents' house. I'd also begun to build a real infrastructure in Wilmington to do this. I'd started a foundation that would, in part, benefit special-needs kids in the area. I'd hinted to my agent that if the Washington Mystics made me an offer, I'd be thrilled. DC was just over an hour away by car or train, so if I settled on them, I wouldn't just *feel* at home, I'd practically be there.

In mid-January, I headed to Shanxi, China, to play for their team in the Chinese Basketball Association play-offs. *I can't just be sitting around waiting for a deal to come together,* I realized, *so I may as well go play overseas for the first time ever.* Unfortunately, my Lyme disease symptoms flared up, and I announced that I was leaving China just a few days after I got there.

Part of me worried that I'd gotten sick because of stress. But I knew there was nothing I could do. I told myself to stay balanced, hope for a great outcome, and trust that my agent would negotiate for the best deal possible back home in the States.

Soon it looked increasingly like that deal was going to be with Washington. Since I'd be what they call a "sign and trade," Washington had made a terrific offer to the Chicago Sky, and the Sky was inclined to accept it. Pending a few final details, I was delighted to make the move.

On February 1, 2017, the Washington Mystics announced that they were trading two of their players and their first-round draft pick in order to acquire me.

"I'm worth three players?" I joked. "Seriously? Does that mean I have to play three times as hard?"

All kidding aside, I might have to. While the Mystics had a terrific coaching staff, including head coach and general manager Mike Thibault, plus amazing record-setting players like Emma Meesseman, they'd won only one play-off series in their nineteen-year history. And that was in 2002! But they'd recently made a few major changes, and I was confident that those shifts would help the team turn around. The owners had just added Kristi Toliver from the championship-winning Los Angeles Sparks, plus re-signed their star guard, Tayler Hill. Making the two of them and me starters would balance out their lineup so that everyone on the court would be a top player. I couldn't wait to join these women.

Most important, the entire coaching and administrative staff were more optimistic than any team I'd been a part of in my life. In the first minute of his press conference announcing that I'd be joining the Mystics, Coach Thibault didn't say we'd be taking baby steps to have a winning season, or that maybe we'd turn things around in a few years. He set his goal sky-high, saying right away that he wanted to seize a championship as soon as possible.

I like that confidence. I don't want growing pains anymore. I'm ready to be bold, and looking forward to the future, I'm determined we'll win. Rebuilding a team from the ground up is an opportunity I can't wait to tackle, and taking home the WNBA Championship trophy is a goal I can't wait to reach.

It will take balance, hard work, positivity, and knowing that whatever life throws my way, I'm ready to meet it. I'll demand excellence in my life, and I know, without a doubt, I'll make it happen.

Afterword

I had a pretty strong feeling that 2017 was going to be the most exciting year of my life, and I was right. I had recently moved to a new apartment outside of DC; I won my first preseason game with the Mystics; and in November, Amanda and I got married!

Honestly, I don't think I've ever been so busy, but my whole crazy up-and-down life has taught me how to balance, so I'm handling it—most of the time. Just like any normal person, sometimes I'm so stressed out or overwhelmed that I break down in tears, hide under the covers, or just want to run away, but I know the feeling will pass. I always tell myself: *This is nothing. You've been through worse. Just keep calm and do your best to juggle it all.*

Being closer to home has been so nice, and I feel like I'm strengthening my bond with Lizzie all over again. Living apart from her has always been hard, but it was doubly so when I was in Chicago. I went home less because I traveled so much already and because hopping on a flight for a one- or two-day trip just wasn't practical. Now I can drive two hours or take a train—and if you know anything about DC traffic, you know that's usually a lot faster!—and I'm back home in Delaware. She and I can hang out on her couch, holding hands or just sitting in silence, for as long as we want.

I can tell already that Lizzie's happier. She has always been such a joyful person, but now she's smiling even more. She seems more at peace. When she squeezes my hand on one of our walks, I can feel how much it means to her that I'm by her side. All Lizzie wants to do is give back to me—or anyone she loves—and that kind of unselfishness is something I want to mirror in my own life.

It's easy to forget to be giving. Too many of us are so busy studying, working, running from one place to another, doing activities, staring into our phones, or collapsing onto our couches to watch TV at the end of the day that we often feel we don't have time to help another person. Worse, we often forget how precious—and endangered—the world we live in is. We pollute, we don't recycle, we don't volunteer, and we spend our money rather than giving it to someone who needs it more than we do.

Lizzie has never taken more than she can give. With every smile, hug, and touch, she is sending love out into the world, and she has taught me that you *have* to be a positive influence on the world and those around you. I'm striving to do that in everything I do.

A few years ago Amanda, our friend Megan, and I began a custom furniture business. Megan had always been into woodworking, but she was making only decorative pieces like wall art. I loved her stuff, and one day a light bulb went off in my head.

We can start a business! Together we're now building coffee and dining tables, sideboards, and art, and even making cutting boards and cheese boards. We sell them on my website, and we do everything in our spare time (ha!), but I can't describe how wonderful it all feels. Not only does crafting and building shut off all the crazy chatter in my head, but I love that our products prove that great furniture doesn't have to be mass-produced overseas, like most companies do. It can be a homemade labor of love, from a tiny business like ours. We don't overcharge for our products, and hopefully soon we'll be hiring people to help us out. In our small way, we're giving back.

I gave back at my and Amanda's wedding, too—an event that could have easily been frivolous and wasteful if I had wanted it to be.

After Amanda and I announced our engagement, the wedding website The Knot chose us as their "Dream Couple." We were the first same-sex couple they'd ever picked, and they committed to featuring our wedding online and in media in exchange for us using their services and helping to promote them. We didn't partner with them out of vanity, though. Trust me, getting more media was *not* what Amanda and I were looking for.

We want people to know that your wedding can be a way to donate back to causes that are important to you. We didn't accept gifts at our wedding, but instead we asked guests to give to the Elena Delle Donne Foundation, which benefits Lyme disease research and special-needs individuals. The Knot publicized my foundation, so just by getting married and working with them, I helped to raise awareness for my favorite causes.

Amanda and I also partnered with a wedding planner who used as many recycled or reused items as possible, plus created minimal waste, so that we reduced our carbon footprint. I wanted our guests to have a blast, but I didn't want it to be at the expense of our precious natural resources. We don't have much time on this earth, so we all need to work together to protect it.

2017 was a year of change, but it was all good. I can't wait for what comes next. I used to be scared that if I did too much, too fast, I'd either lose sight of what was driving me or I'd burn out entirely. I don't feel that way anymore. I've learned to listen to myself, trust others, work as part of a team, pursue realistic goals while still dreaming big, and learn how to balance. If I do all of those things, tackling big changes feels like an opportunity rather than a challenge.

I hope this book has helped you find ways to do the same. If there's anything I wish for you, it's that you'll know that if you make mistakes or can't accomplish something, it's not the end of the world. When I left UConn, I thought basketball was over for me. But here I am, not even thirty, and I've won an Olympic gold medal and risen to the top of the WNBA. Life has unfolded for me in ways I never would have expected, and I know it will do the same in the future—for me *and* for you.

Always demand excellence. Chances are, you'll get it.

Acknowledgments

I have a team of people that I would like to thank, and I fully recognize that I would not be where I am today without the support of my family and friends behind me.

Amanda, my wife and my best friend, you have given up and sacrificed so much to help me better my career (even being my off-season workout partner). Words cannot express how much you mean to me, and I am so excited that you are with me for life. We are a pretty unstoppable team.

Special thanks to my incredible parents, who have been with me since day one. Mom, thank you for being extremely honest, absolutely hilarious, and my ultimate role model for what strength looks like. The thankless tasks that you have done day in and day out to support me have never gone unnoticed. I was and still am always watching your lead and am in awe of you.

Dad, thank you for driving me all the way to Pennsylvania twice a week, attending every AAU tournament, and still traveling to lots of my WNBA games. You are my biggest fan. And by the way, thanks for teaching me how to shoot a basketball—it's been pretty helpful in my professional career (Dr. Evil hand motion <3).

To my older sister, Lizzie, thank you for helping me keep everything in perspective. You remind me that there is so much more to life and that joys can come from anywhere; even something as simple as the wind or a perfectly cooked rib eye. You are the greatest gift to our family.

Thanks to my big brother, Gene, for being able to make me laugh, especially through the lows, and for being my biggest cheerleader. My love of the game started because of you. Playing minny ball until we dropped, going to brutal workouts together; any goal seemed attainable with you by my side. Jennifer, thank you for keeping me trendy and bringing me one of the greatest joys of my life, Gia. To Gia, thank you for bringing so much light into our family and for being the outlet from basketball that I need every once in a while. You are constantly motivating me to be a better role model. Please never stop calling me Ewena.

Aunt Jan and Aunt Jill, thanks for providing me with comedic relief and constant support during this entire journey. I hope I can be half the aunt to Gia that you have both been to me. My uncles, thank you for trying to tame big Ern through games and still following so closely throughout my career. Your encouraging texts and words mean so much to me.

Dave, my grandfather/uncle/brother/playmate. "Man Greens . . . you're good lookin." My constant one-on-one buddy and arm tickler, thanks for letting me start my career as an author in your workout books. The days of knee football prepared me for anything I'd ever see in the pros.

Kim, the best babysitter a girl could ever ask for. A.k.a. Kimothy Kathedral. Thank you for putting up with watching the same movie fifty times in a row (Dunston Checks In) and for being my true childhood best friend. God blessed us with two angels when he gave us Lizzie and also sent you into our lives.

To my trainer, John Noonan, thank you for being more than a trainer, and for being my friend. You are always able to read exactly what I need at the right time, whether it is a crazy workout or just going to P.F. Chang's.

Wrigley, my greatest friend and Greatest Dane. Thanks for being my rock in Chicago and for attacking me with love every time I come home. Rasta, thanks for being the edge and sass in our home and for being the only one in our house who can keep Amanda in check.

Thank you, Meghan, for being a goofball with me in college, for making me laugh until I cried, for being my secret keeper and my sounding board for everything. And to Marge, when Meghan was boring, thank you for taking over.

Tamika Catchings, thank you for being the best role model I could look up to the second I got into the league. By watching you, it made me better. I will never forget the first time I played against you and you sent a forearm straight to my chest. It was a solid welcome to the WNBA. You were a permanent reminder that I needed to get stronger.

To Jacki Gemelos, my MVP season would not have happened without you by my side.

Erin Kane and Alyssa Romano, thank you for helping me discover myself and for helping me find my voice. This wouldn't have happened without the greatest team behind me.

Sarah Durand, you are a rock star. Thank you.

Thanks to Octagon literary agent Jennifer Keene for all her great work on this project. Thanks to the all-stars at Simon & Schuster, including Liz Kossnar.

Thank you all.